The Art of Connectivity

The Art of Connectivity

A Call for Unity
Within a Diverse Society

Melvin Markell McPhearson

authorHOUSE®

AuthorHouse™
1663 Liberty Drive
Bloomington, IN 47403
www.authorhouse.com
Phone: 1-800-839-8640

First published by AuthorHouse   06/14/ 2011

ISBN: 978-1-4634-1066-7 (sc)
ISBN: 978-1-4634-1065-0 (dj)
ISBN: 978-1-4634-1064-3 (ebk)

Library of Congress Control Number: 2011909337

Printed in the United States of America

Any people depicted in stock imagery provided by Thinkstock are models, and such images are being used for illustrative purposes only.
Certain stock imagery © Thinkstock.

This book is printed on acid-free paper.

CONTENTS

FOREWORD

Connecting to Christ, the center of life for all Christians, is the most crucial and demanding goal to be pursued. Melvin Markell McPhearson has written this book in hopes that many persons will read it, use it as a personal study aid, and also decide to make it a resource for youth and adults in their congregations.

I met Markell about a decade ago when he matriculated at Virginia Union University to study for the Master of Divinity degree. From the beginning I sensed his passion for leading people to change their lifestyles. He spoke often of his belief that something more was needed than what was being taught in seminaries and practiced in churches if persons were to live a life of service in obedience to the call of Christ. Believing that the answer lay in the church's teaching, Markell chose to pursue the Christian education track in the Master of Divinity (M. Div.) curriculum. Thus it came as no surprise when he contacted me to share the work he hoped would be used by pastors and lay leaders.

The Art of Connectivity is Markell's attempt to bring unity to the key leaders in the church. In his first chapter he explains what he means by "connectivity" and suggests that we need to get rid of negative behaviors that contribute to the prevalent state of disconnection. Chapter two outlines the challenge he would keep ever before us: to do what we know we should do, in love and obedience to Christ. The next four chapters present various perspectives that will help one see, perceive, and be able to do self-analysis leading to connectivity. In chapter nine we are admonished to "seek ways of connecting to others." To be connected lovingly to others is to be connected to God, our ultimate aim.

Gloria C. Taylor, Ed.D

Dr. Taylor is the Director of Christian Education at the Samuel DeWitt Proctor School of Theology at Virginia Union University in Richmond, Virginia.

Acknowledgment

To my parents, Charles Lindbergh McPhearson Sr. (deceased) and Pearlean McPhearson (deceased), who nurtured and directed my steps in the Lord.

To my wife, Antoinette McPhearson, thank you for assisting me in completing this project during some late nights and some long days, weeks, months, and through the years. I pray that God will enlarge our territory as He opens ministry opportunities to us to reach the lost and those who are seeking enlightenment and spiritual transformation through Christian education.

To our five children, Monique Jasmine, Brodrick Deondre, Ashley Nicole, Jozef Markell, and Malika Michelle, for allowing me this time to study and to write.

To my brothers and sisters, Patricia, Charles, Carolyn, Keith, Donald, Debra, Michael, Byron, LaShaun, and Anthony, who helps me to maintain my centeredness.

To Doctors, Mary McFarland-McPherson (Aunt Mary), and Gloria C. Taylor encouragers with love and compassion, Thank you for assisting in the editing of my dissertation, this manuscript and providing constructive comments.

To my personal family members, uncles, aunts, cousins, to my spiritual family, to Pastor Wesley Keith McLaughlin and to all whom I have encountered in my spiritual journey, especially those who are now asleep but remain alive in my heart, in my stories, and on these pages.

To those whom I have sinned against either by omission or commission, forgive me; and may we find ways of reconnecting in the body of the Lord. May the Lord continually connect and maintain the living upon His solid foundation. May He connect believers physically and spiritually beyond what their eyes may see, their ears may hear, and their intellect may understand.

Lastly, but certainly not least, to my heavenly Father, who opens and closes doors at His discretion. Thank you for opening the windows of heaven and allowing a stable bridge to be built across the troubled waters in my life.

You have connected me in relationships and built a solid foundation that is accessible for stability in my life despite my weakness. Your faithfulness has restored my faith; Father, you are continually connecting me and making me whole. Thank you.

Introduction

Connectivity and Eradicating Negativity

"People can live together in unity, while embracing theirs and others' cultural values."—M. Markell McPhearson

Life is too short to not live it to its fullness or to not enjoy it each and every day. Because longevity is not guaranteed, I emphatically believe we should work together to reclaim biblical connectivity. The dreams of Dr. Martin Luther King Jr., John Wesley, Mahatma Gandhi, Rev. Dr. Floyd Flake, Rev. Dr. Wyatt T. Walker, John Calvin, and many others impel us to move forward to restore honor in all aspects of our lives. We must envision positive new beginnings, and honor that which is not fueled by divisions. Throughout history, there have been examples of many who have rallied with good intentions and we must not forget that which is noble and honorable. Nevertheless, because connectivity was not always placed on the table, some have sprinkled seeds of separation, self-hatred, and negativity in our midst. Therefore, this writing serves to assist individuals to recognize negative and destructive behavioral traits within themselves and in others. Recognizing negativity in a proactive manner is the first step in embracing positive behavioral traits. This writing seeks to guide individuals toward accepting themselves, their ethnicity, those from their native land, and those in the Diaspora (people living outside their country of origin). Also, this writing embraces those in their personal context and eventually all men, women, boys, and girls regardless of their ethnicity. Lastly, this writing serves to embrace theological, biblical, historical, psychological and sociological perspectives through Christian education and holistically connecting with one another.

It is God's calling that has inspired this writing to serve and connect oneself holistically, and to build upon relationships and traditional values in the church that are biblical. It is God's calling to negate traditional doctrines, hatred, unjust separations, and occurrences that are not biblical, which may serve to subdue and hold believers and non-believers in a state of delusional bondage. This writing serves to help those in the church (and in the world) to eradicate self-negation and family separation. Nevertheless, it has to be said that total eradication will never occur, but each of us must be willing to eliminate negative circumstances for the betterment of who we are as well as all mankind. This writing also serves to allow others to see caring families fostering a community of sharing, working, studying, and praying together in a loving (holistic), family / communal relationship.

Whereas I do not condone prejudices and disruptive behavioral traits, I assert that all ethnicities must see and embrace the known and the unknown values in their history and in biblical history. When societies personally embrace their ethnicity, they will be better aligned to healthily embrace other ethnicities without opposing their social order or other way of life. It is further emphasized that if ethnicities dare to embrace these values, they may be aligned to help themselves, their families, their congregations, and the communities in which they serve to see Godly values in all people. It is also important to know that after the aforementioned has been embraced, many may then be able to live together in harmony, and thereby live life to the fullness established by the Architect of this universe since the beginning of human conception.

The question may be asked, How can we work together to eradicate or minimize oppositional forces that negate one's ability to move forward productively? This question has plagued the American people for hundreds of years. It is in American history where you may find stories of religious and educational segregation, racial divisions, social and economic unrest, and many other abnormalities. So, how do we agree to disagree, while leaving the conversation with hope and perhaps glimpses of another perspective, belief, or possibility—without verbal and physical confrontations? How do we come to the realization that *all men* are created equal and were created in the image of the Almighty God? How can we begin to sit at tables, or live in shared homes or communities, one with another, in a genuine effort to understand each other without prejudice? These questions are merely a start to open minds through connectivity, questions that prayerfully would serve as templates to bring godly men, women, boys, and girls together in oneness.

An essential focus of this writing is connecting and evangelizing the local community through Christian educational methodologies. It is calling individuals and church leaders to address the plight of illegal activities, and negating circumstances in churches and in the local community through Christian education training and evangelism. It is time-out for churches to be built in communities where degradation and non-productive activities are allowed to exist without individuals, churches, community colleges, and local law enforcement agencies working together as dynamic lines of defense. No one should be denied productive opportunities in life for whatever reasons—especially due to poverty, crime, unproductive forces, and a lack of quality education (biblical and secular). Individuals and churches must be proactive in searching out numerous opportunities for communal and self-help improvements; with this others may be able to free themselves through spiritual developmental and educational methodologies.

God has called this writing into the educational process of self-help and self-awareness, a process introduced to the writer by the president of Virginia University of Lynchburg, Dr. Ralph Reaves. Some African Americans and other ethnic groups have been misguided concerning false religious practices and some traditional values of their ancestors, of their society, and their religion. There was a time when strong African/ethnic beliefs kept the people in close relationships with one another; this is one reason the African proverb resounds worldwide, "It takes a village to raise a child." This proverb speaks to individuals, families, and communal value systems that were instilled in families—systems that I believe have been lost in many communities. The proverb's value serves to instill self-help and self-awareness, therefore it is advantageous to all individuals and families to embrace and teach the meaning of the African proverb to assist in the nurturing of the child and the village (home and community).

I am moved by intellectual history, personal stories, meaningful songs, and festive dancers in the Spirit. It is drummers and the musician's instrumental compellations, it is those who are adorned with beautiful and vibrant colors of clothing, it is the magnificent and well-crafted jewelry, and the developmental commitment to a spiritual relationship with God, which I believe are evidences of what I call, "The African/ethnic connection," within my experience and personal context.

Therefore, as other believers are connected and reconnected through Christian education, basic academic studies and possibly higher education, lives will be restored and doors will be opened. Education must be a vital part of every Christian life. Either one is properly educated, or he/she is miss-educated (improperly trained) or uneducated (not trained). Theological concerns in individuals' lives are addressed in the church and in the local community through this format, so others may grow spiritually and understand their condition of existence. Christian educational training in self-awareness, self-help, and interdependence is also essential to one's wholeness. Some may rise up and say, "The Holy Ghost is my teacher and all that educational stuff is not needed." Well, let me say that God has given believers the Holy Ghost, the Holy Bible, *and* theological and biblical educational tools to assist all believers to grow and know the truth that will set them free. *Study to show thyself approved* is a biblical phrase that should be taken seriously in the church, and believers should study and not just depend on the Holy Spirit to give them revelation. Through proper teaching, individuals and leaders will be enlightened concerning the Christ while building upon their spiritual, physical, and ancestral lives. This enlightenment will be accomplished through active participation in learning experiences, which cause one to delve within the teachings of those who have lived and died so *all people* can live together in unity, while embracing their own and other's cultural values.

Individuals and leaders must join hands to work in harmony, to comfort those in pain and to celebrate with those who are rejoicing. Many churches have served as a ray of light to those who are in dark and chaotic conditions. Local churches must not only build larger buildings, but they must be active participants in building holistic lives within their walls and within the community where they are situated.

I am a visionary who continues to find and see God in every aspect of life. I believe wherever God places a church, that church is equipped to serve and be intrinsically involved in the community. As the church becomes the heart of the community, the church and the community must thrive together holistically. The moral values of children, teens, adults, families, and our nation have deteriorated. They have been compromised by some who are misguided in our society, in some churches, and through some religious and civil leaders. Holistic values established in community churches may be the last defensive line of protection available before Satan and his demons are invited in by some to kill, steal, and destroy our children, our families, our churches, and eventually our nation. Godly leaders and church members are called to unite to "fight the good fight of the faith"[1] and to connect one with another to accomplish God's purpose for not only the churches but for all of humanity as well.

It is asserted that God, Christian education training, and the military, have equipped (and are equipping) me as the writer of this book to fight on the front lines of Christianity in what I see as an ongoing spiritual warfare. I am continually redefining my present theological knowledge as I reflect upon my past, present, and future studies. Consequently, my basic convictions and understanding of personal theology in the Diaspora is ever changing. I know others—and there will be others still—who share in carrying the torch of liberation and social justice. It is imperative that we are liberated from ignorance, personal prejudices, and verbal hatred, and that we hold ourselves and others accountable for wrongs allowed to statically exist in our society. Therefore, I am calling all torchbearers forward to accomplish the work of God in their homes, in their churches, in their communities, and in the uttermost parts of the world so that light would be illuminated, and dark and chaotic behaviors would be diminish and eventually be eradicated.

As torches are carried into local communities and to all nations, truth will be proclaimed and eventually prevail like justice rolling from mighty streams of truth, justice, freedom, and liberation. As truth prevails, it will be embraced by many (through Christian and secular education methodologies and cultural history), and the people will become connected to the holistic bodies of baptized believers; bodies that embrace all people regardless of their creed, nationality, color, ethnicity, or anything that may serve to separate them from the love of God Almighty.

Leaders who are endowed with godly love and who are devoted to their churches have love like that of mothers who give birth. The mother loves and nurtures the child or children in her care. She loves them from conception unto death, and church leaders must be like-minded. Leaders must embrace those in their care, and individuals must be nurtured to live in a holistic and loving community without being relegated to simply being a person who is voted in as a member (receiving the right hand of

---

[1]   I Timothy 6:12a, NRSV.

fellowship) and then left alone to fend for themselves without proper love, nurture, and direction.

For centuries, separation and negativism have been part of the African American heritage and legacy his forefathers left as the writer's truth—or untruth—through written or verbal *his-story* and stories. At times, it is as if African-Americans evolved from thin air, or from the bowels and cries of the inhumane slave ships, auction blocks, and plantations scattered throughout the United States of America, the land of the free.

African-Americans and all ethnicities must delve into the educational process and search for biblical and secular educational truth. In finding truth, we will know without a doubt who we are and from whence we came according not only to stories that have been handed down from generation to generation but according to biblical and secular education as well.

Steps Toward Connectivity and Eradicating Negativity

1. *How can you embrace connectivity in your context without negating others and what are some negating circumstances in your context?*

2. *How should you work with others to reclaim biblical connectivity and restore honor to build upon relationships and traditional values?*

3. *How can you work toward eradicating self-negation, seeing caring families sharing, working, studying, and praying in loving and holistic relationships?*

4. *How can you embrace the African proverb, "It takes a village to raise a child," and embrace and love those in your care?*

5. *Why should you embrace your personal ethnicity before embracing other ethnicities?*

6. *How do you agree to disagree without prejudice? How do you leave the conversation with hope as well as glimpses of another perspective, belief, or possibility, without verbal and physical confrontations?*

7. *What can you do to effectively evangelize the local community through Christian educational methodologies?*

8. *What can you do to address illegal activities, while negating their effects in churches and in your local community?*

9. *How can you effectively embrace Christian education, self-awareness, self-help, and interdependence?*

10. *It is imperative that you are liberated from ignorance, personal prejudices, and verbal hatred. How can you carry the torch of liberation and address social justice in your context?*

The Art of Connectivity

"Connectivity is wholeness, healthiness, and spiritual well—being one with another."
"We are a breath of wind, a glimmer of light, a whisper in a dark and distant night. We are one, connected to accomplish that which is not always simple, but that which is right".—M. Markell McPhearson

The Art of Connectivity begins as an individual quest. This entails finding oneself and becoming whole and healthy, only then will one be able to assist others holistically and without prejudice. Personal connectivity is attempting to fulfill the lyrics Diana Ross sang, "Do you know where you're going to? Do you like the things that life is showing you? Where are you going to? Do you know . . ."[2] Connectivity is wholeness, healthiness, and spiritual well-being (holistic well-being) as an individual as well as one with another.

Connectivity is a bridge over uncertainty. It is a compass on untraveled roads. It is the glue that binds and re-connects families, friends, and communities. It is true love in action. Connectivity involves knowing who you are as well as knowing your intended purpose in life. Connectivity is mapping your life backward and securing direction and re-direction throughout that life journey. Connectivity is staying in your lane at times, or crossing and eradicating negative and chaotic lines as the Holy Spirit inspires you. Connectivity is helping others after you have helped yourself

---

[2]   Theme from *Mahogany (Do You Know Where You're Going To)*. Lyrics by Michael Masser and Gerald Goffin.

or found help from the hands of another. It is helping oneself and opening doors so others may be helped.

Therefore, I write of connectivity in an attempt to unite the disconnected. I write in a world where we are all really one, separated by our fears, our stories, our languages, our religions, our race, and our ethnicity. I write to bring together fraternities, sororities, political parties, faith groups, those separated by social lines and a host of other commonalities we use to unite or separate us from one another. I write for the child who has no clothes, the abused woman who has no voice, and the man who has been negated by ignorance, hatred, and prejudice. I write so the unseen, the unheard, and the underprivileged may be connected. I also write because in times of trouble we often find common ground where we are connected. When somber circumstances like wars, life stresses, and natural disasters are before us, it seems like it is then that we are connected and re-connected, one to another, and we serve those who are in need. So, I write of the dangerous, dark, and chaotic experiences, and the stories that disconnect us from one another. I write about widening gaps and of coming together in oneness.

If one finds himself, realizes his spiritual value and intended purpose in life, he is less likely to be self-destructive. Likewise, if one is connected holistically and knows what one has been called or created to do, then one can map out one's life and take the appropriate detours when obstacles arise. On the other hand, if one is living only with undefined directions and focus, one may become lost, unstable, or unable to move ahead when a detour or obstacle is encountered. Proven Christian and secular educational processes and methodologies are vital in selecting the holistic vehicles that propel an individual or group from disdainful situations to the state of connectivity.

Many biblical theologians have written that man (Adam) was disconnected due to a disobedient nature, and he was eventually evicted from the Garden of Eden.[3] From that time, men and women have been spiritually disconnected. They may be on a quest to find themselves and their connections with others by which they may align themselves and establish themselves with their God, whereby a true spiritual walk in the universe is realized. Others may say connecting to God, to others, and spiritually to everything that is good are the only true connections in

---

[3]   Genesis 3:22-24, RSV.

this present life. Regardless of your preference, know that connectivity is essential to your wholeness and living harmoniously for the betterment of all in this world. Begin now and ask yourself, Do I know who I am? Do I know where I am going? Am I prepared for the journey? If I am not prepared for the journey, am I willing to ask for help? Am I willing to change in a positive manner and become spiritually aligned to assist others to see the true and vibrant light that was established by the Master of this universe?

Positive connections have allowed others to live holistically within their particular faith practices, in the richness found in their particular heritage, within their families, and in their communities, towns, and villages. In this writing, the village represents a personal commitment that holistically fosters wellness to those who reside in the local community. In the Holy Bible, Rahab, Esther, and the original apostles of Jesus Christ are examples of persons who found direction in their villages and later assisted others holistically. Ancestors such as Joseph and Moses were used to help others see their positive and spiritual connections in life, to their God, to one another, and at times they used their leadership skills to help others remain in alliance;[4] this writing is no different.

This writing is one effort that can be used to assist others to embrace the art of connectivity (godly connections). Connectivity may be seen through biblical leaders (such as Moses, David, Paul, or Jesus Christ), as well as through historical leaders (such as Mahatma Gandhi, Dr. Martin Luther King Jr., or Mother Teresa), who served to liberate others from negative circumstances. These leaders knew the value of positive connections without egotism, prejudice, and self-pride. They understood that keeping people connected and liberated from poverty and self-destruction would serve to enrich the lives of all individuals involved, including future generations.

Upon delving into this connection, and for the betterment of future generations, positive changes must be meticulously taken as acts of peace, love, hope, and happiness while illuminating the positive aspects of connectivity and embracing one's heritage. Through learned behavior, some have not been taught to recognize, value, or appreciate persons of their past. These practices have caused some to not embrace others or their

---

4   Exodus 1:1-7 (Joseph connection), and I King 6:12-13 (David and the children of Israel connection).

heritage, their connectivity, or themselves. They are often vehemently opposed to having any close affiliation with their heritage, their past, or with others who are not like them. It is this writer's belief that those who live in the Diaspora and refuse to embrace their heritage, who negate their relational connection to their country (whether in Africa, Europe, Asia, the Americas, and so on), understandably have a sense of self-negation and self-destruction.

If people contradict their past, they may intentionally or unintentionally assimilate other ethnicities so that they may assume to be someone other than who they were intended to be in life or who God created them to be in this world. Through this assimilation process, they may become people who have little or no tie to those who struggled and died to preserve their lives and their heritage in the midst of chaotic predicaments. They will negate the traditional clothing and languages of their ancestors, and in many ways become like those who negated their very existence. In most cases, the self-negated person's identity may be forever lost in a "melting pot" that only embraces some customs and traditions, while negating others.[5] Thus one's original ethnic ties with this country may be negative in nature. Such ties may reveal ancestors who were born in the belly of a disease-infested slave ship or on a torturous slave plantation, who were sold on the slave market as mere commodities, who served as indentured servants, or who faced other adversities. Others may see their ties in drug-infested families, criminal circumstances, violence, or in a life of mishap and dilapidated state of affairs. In any of these cases, covert and overt psychological behavioral traits are asserted as one elevates European values or other ethnic values within a society of racial unrest.

Nevertheless, one must make peace with his or her past to prevent carrying luggage (hurts) from the past.[6] As one realizes the Almighty was present with his or her ancestors whose history is captured in their particular biblical writings, one's perspective is refocused toward positive spiritual and physical connections. There is a refocus in one's understanding, through those who came before him; one's physical and spiritual strength is reinforced. In this understanding one may rise to greatness in the midst of chaotic laws and prejudiced minds that seek to negate people of color,

---

[5]   Tamar Jacoby, *Reinventing the Melting Pot—The New immigrants and What It Means to Be American* (New York: Basic Books, 2004).

[6]   H. Norman Wright, *Making Peace with Your Past* (Ada, MI: Revell, 1985).

be it red, yellow, black, white, or any color under the sun. But know that through the art of connectivity, one may rise spiritually, holistically, and healthily by mapping one's life backward, embracing self-awareness and spiritual gifts, and one's ancestral heritage.

With the exception of a major disaster or catastrophe, self-negated people are disconnected people who have demonstrated a denial of self and self-destructive attitude toward themselves, toward others, and toward their past. Look at the woman who would let a man or another use her so that she may be accepted if only for a moment. Look at the man who is destructive toward himself and others because his self-worth has not been realized or validated. These are negative behaviors associated with negative self-identity that has been taught and perpetrated throughout history and/or has been carried from one generation to another. Destructive mentalities have plagued and separated many disconnected people for hundreds or possibly thousands of years.

I emphatically assert that there are those who have in many ways associated themselves and their beginnings with the tormenting slave castles, poverty, inhumane conditions, slave ships, and violent slave plantations of their ancestral past, which once stretched across many continents. Some have been ridiculed, stripped of their original faith practices, their families, their names, their respective dialects, and their clothing. It is my belief that all of this occurred as overt psychological warfare tactics; warlike strategies were implemented for command and control, although a declaration of war was never signed into law. This was accomplished in an environment—which some call slave castles, prisons, slave plantations, and many other names throughout the world—where thousands were taken as prisoners, enslaved, murdered, raped, tortured, and inhumanely treated in hundreds of prisoner of war camps.

Despite these atrocities, a positive reconnection may assimilate a healthy and holistic environment. We must understand our heritage and our theology, utilizing self-awareness and interdependent approaches. This transformative approach includes embracing one another, hearing the voices of those who have given their lives for equality and liberation, while embracing and introducing the healing process to those who remain disconnected. In an effort to map one's life backward, an individual must embrace a positive vision of oneself in the future, and then work diligently to attain a healthy and productive lifestyle. This individual must now not only see the vision, but he or she must embrace the vision while averting or recovering holistically from obstacles in their path. As individuals we must learn what some of my Ghanaian brothers have often said, "Every climber needs a push," or as I say, every dark circumstance needs a torchbearer to give light to dark situations for one to be successful in life.

Oftentimes, it is the negative learned behavior traits (disorders) that are displayed in one's community, demeanors, and in one's attitudes, which must be deprogrammed or re-mapped and positive countermeasures implemented. This implementation serves to overtake and destroy negativism; it is negativism that has caused some people, such as people of color and those who are poverty stricken, to negate themselves, their rich heritage, and the voices of faithful servants of the past and the present.

We must move forward to unveil positive countermeasures to deter negative behaviors and actions. The positive counteractions are primarily the responsibility of the individual to accept and implement, but it is also a shared responsibility of churches, religious organizations, political organizations, the laity, local communities, villages, and worldwide leaders. This shared responsibility must be transmitted and put into action by any positive or holistic means necessary to assist the self-negated to become connected and productive members of society. Just as so many pull together and work together during a major disaster for the good of all concerned, we must see the signs of destruction in others and we must help rescue those who desire to be rescued. Such connectivity would assist and elevate one to realize and embrace who they are while connecting one with many to stand united. This also would alleviate a person's dependence on another person or system, which may perpetuate partial dependency or a "blanket" mentality, thereby in many ways covering up one's infested wounds and weaknesses without giving adequate treatment to one's serious illness. This writer asserts that an internal wound that has not been treated properly may appear healthy, but over time the remaining internal damage heightens the infested situation. Therefore, this shared responsibility of assisting and educating the downtrodden is a necessity that serves to implement self-awareness and interdependence through connectivity, formal education, and Christian educational methodologies.

I have determined that a deeper problem exists within those who have caused and continue to cause wounds to be opened and reopened, as individuals reside and work within particular environments. At some point, those who are causing such wounds to remain open must address their participation and the participation of their ancestors in such malevolent behavior. This will serve to expedite the healing process of those who may have wanted to give up, as well as those who recognize their continual abuse at their own hands, or of a perceived ancestral given right.

In many ways, some have been taught by certain segments of society that nothing good can or could possibly come from an individual, a family, a community, or a country. Nevertheless, self-awareness and holistic healing will assist persons in disconnected positions and those whom they serve. Self-awareness and holistic healing must be offered to all individuals involved on all sides of the spectrum as we suffer and rejoice with one another, not only in our particular family, community, or society but also throughout the world. Finally, this writing has inspired me to delve into further research and to continue assisting individuals and leaders to get connected to God and to become foundationally grounded in the body of Christ. With this in mind, Maya Angelou's pledge (see Appendix A) is offered as a reminder to all persons in the African American community and beyond.

Steps Toward Navigating Your Life

1. *Start by making a plan for your life. Write down your short-term plans (up to one year); now write down your mid-term plans (one year to five years); lastly write down your long-term plans (five to twenty years and beyond).*

2. *Write down what you believe to be your intended purpose in life.*

3. *Take your answers from questions one and two and make a road map of how you plan to map your life backward to secure direction throughout your life journey. You may need to develop several maps, for example, educational, family, spiritual, financial, employment, and so on.*

4. *Write down negative and positive attributes about yourself and develop interventions to assist you in eradicating negative attributes/ behavioral traits.*

5. Write down the people who will assist you to stay in your lane as you navigate potholes, obstacles, and some negative and chaotic lines in your life.

6. Write down the name of at least one person you can offer a helping hand, and ways you can help the person(s). Consider seniors and children to whom you can offer help.

7. Start or join a prayer/support group (no more than twenty people and/ or ten couples) to assist you in staying on course. Now pray without ceasing!

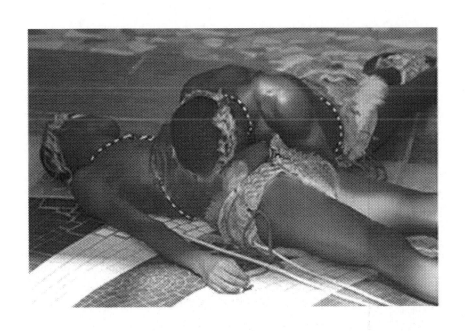

The Challenge

"When we know better, we must do better for the betterment of all people in this world. This is that which cannot be lost!"—M. Markell McPhearson

The challenge is offered as a perspective that is hardly confined to one region. This challenge may be found within the boundaries of any city, town, village, or community throughout the world. Simply put, many of the sociocultural abnormalities that are nebulous to some of my readers and residents of any community will be cleared if individuals, the local communities, and leaders would simply get connected, listen, hear, and work with one another for the betterment of the people they serve and love. Love is an essential force in any and all healthy relationships. Love is the "more excellent way" expressed in the book of First Corinthians. True love serves to connect believers and unbelievers to unite and work together for the betterment of all involved. It is the power of agape love that propels and challenges believers and unbelievers down paths of connectivity, to live together peacefully and positively.

Therefore, correcting economical, educational, and criminal challenges that plague the world are within the reach of any and all communities if self-awareness and connectivity are properly addressed and presented in a positive manner. Some have served as a ray of light and hope to those who were living in dark and chaotic circumstances; today this challenge is no different. We must cease from ministering and embracing solely those whom we feel we are connected to in life, and embrace one another worldwide without prejudice.

In the past, many churches and religious organizations were viable entities in the African American community. While there are churches and organizations that are intricately involved in their local communities today, there are others that are not relevant entities in their communities. Churches and other organizations must be resurrected as refuges for the people of their communities, and they must be involved in evangelizing others around the world. It is time for church leaders to build Christian educational centers and schools and to curtail building larger sanctuaries and fellowship halls. It is time for Christian education scholarships to be in the forefront (or equally placed) of church scholarship programs. It is past time for Christian education to be embraced in every aspect of ministry and woven throughout the personal lives it touches.

It is in the church and in local and national organizations where many will find hope in education and through spiritual and religious educational enrichment programs. The church (through Christian education) is where many learned of their heritage and where formal education took place for many years. Since many schools did not teach or were not allowed to teach African American (Black or Negro) history, it is in the church that people learned the songs of their heritage, their culture, and other historical events that helped so many persevere during difficult times. It is also in the church where many people heard, theologically, how it would be possible for them to endure whatever they were facing in their condition of existence. The people were taught they could and would endure, especially since so many from Africa and others from the plantations (prisoner of war camps) paved the way and endured to the end.

Despite the many obstacles that were and are presented, people around the world have been educated and have obtained that which others have attempted to keep from them. Once we know better, we must do better for the advancement of all people in this world. This is that which cannot be lost! We must be able to map out our destination intellectually amidst the verbal and written words of yesterday and in this present time. Lastly, as it was the presidential campaign theme of President Barack Obama, let us say with our heads held high amidst those who lived and died for justice and freedom, "Yes We Can, Yes We Can, Yes We Can!"

Steps Toward Embracing Challenges in Your Context

1. *What are some negative or chaotic challenges and some* sociocultural *abnormalities* (**social** experiences and cultural values) *that exist in your context or community?*

2. *What are the economical, educational, and criminal challenges that plague your context or community?*

3. *Name steps you can take to correct the challenges that plague your context or community.*

4. *How can Christian educational programs embrace and be woven throughout personal lives in your context or community?*

5. *Theologically speaking, what steps can you take to map out your destination intellectually?*

A Theological Vision Revealed

". . . it is negative attitudes, one's ego, self-pride, and negative behavioral traits (sin) that lead one toward disconnecting oneself from God and others."—M. Markell McPhearson

God is calling His people to return to Him by building upon a solid foundation, getting connected or reconnected to Him and to one another. Theologically, it is negative attitudes, one's ego, self-pride, and negative behavioral traits (sin) that lead one toward disconnecting oneself from God and others, as well as not believing and/or supporting the body of Christ, and disconnecting oneself from one's ethnicity. When God created mankind in His garden and in His image, He did not condone the existence of destructive behavioral traits. It is God's will that all are freed from the bondages of sin, especially since sin is a destructive force that separates God's people from Him. Therefore, it is liberation theology that best describes the condition of existence associated with the downtrodden. "In (James) Cone's view, liberation is the essence of Christianity and Jesus Christ is the liberator."[7] Liberation theology and Black or African-American theology concentrates on social justice issues for those who are underserved and those who have been maltreated by society; it addresses faith communities' particular circumstances, and their past and present circumstances.[8] Since God is a positive God, any form of self-negation, in reality, is an unconstructive attribute that is contrary to

---

[7] James H. Harris, *Pastoral Theology: A Black Church Perspective* (Minneapolis: Fortress Press, 1991), 61.

[8] Owen C. Thomas and Ellen K. Wondra, Introduction to Theology (Harrisburg: Morehouse Publishing 2002), 7-8.

who God is and to who we are—and to who we will become if we embrace the teachings of Jesus Christ and implement positive social practices.

Christian anthropology reflects upon who God is as a person, and who is in relationship with He who created the world. In the world He has created mankind in His image and in His likeness (Imago Dei).[9] Theologically, in the Holy Scriptures we find evidence of being a created being. In the beginning "God created man in His [own] image, in the image of God created He him; male and female created He them."[10] It was God who created man (Adam) in His image in the beginning; man reflected the glory of God before the fall. This writer contends that evil was and is allowed to roam the earth, and after the fall, evil and a negative judgment were placed on man, thereby creating a polarity against mankind based on the fall of man. This theological belief is intrinsic in the concept of being perfected in the image of God.

The theological vision that supports these concerns is found in what some theologians call the division in the Corinthian church (I Corinthians 3:10-15); in the creation story (Genesis 1:1-2:3); in the Great Commission (Matthew 28:16-20); in the proper function of spiritual gifts (I Corinthians 12:1-14:40); and in the building of unity within the body of Christ (Ephesians 4:1-16). In creation, man was created in God's image, in God's likeness, and adorned with the glory of God. In the Great Commission, Jesus commanded his disciples to "Go ye therefore, and teach all nations, baptizing them in the name of the Father, and of the Son, and of the Holy Ghost." As Christians embrace themselves and others and practice the Great Commission, others should come to the knowledge of the Father as they accept the teachings of the Father in their hearts. In recognizing the proper function of spiritual gifts, one should see how the gifts work harmoniously to give God the glory as one builds on the solid foundation and as one is connected through those gifts and holistic Christian educational teaching. Therefore, negative behavior traits and negative attitudes should be forced out as agape love (godly love) is encouraged and forgiveness is fostered. Positive behavior traits and attitudes resonate throughout God's temple (the body of the believer).

---

[9] Donald W. Musser and Joseph L. Price, *A New Handbook of Christian Theology* (2002), 28.

[10] Genesis 1:27, NIV.

The theological problems of assimilating negative attitudes and negative behavioral practices must be evaluated, as they have led so many toward a self-destructive course of self-negation, because that which leads one to disconnect one's self, one's heritage, and one's faith practices manifests itself amid a psychological enslavement of one's mental faculties. As has been previously stated, negative behavior is associated with a negative self-identity that may have been taught throughout history and carried from generation to generation. Therefore, it is asserted that destructive mentalities (self-negation and self-hatred) have plagued minorities and people of color for hundreds if not thousands of years, and the self-negated personal theological mold must be broken and placed on the "potter's wheel" to be reshaped by the Master Potter. But we know God takes care of the spiritual realm, and, from the beginning of creation He has called man forward to take care of the physical realm. Therefore, it is time out for just "bended knee" theology. We must pray, cross theological lines, and work to repair and reshape broken vessels.

Na'im Akbar writes, in his book *Light from Ancient Africa* (chapter two, "Finding the African Self"), that we are "involved in the Western scientific definitional process . . . whereas . . . Western psychologists are concerned with how each of us *differs* from the other. The Ancients, on the other hand, looked at the 'essence of sameness.'"[11] When we realize it is in our sameness, as children of God, that we are given a royal position as joint heirs with Christ, we will love our Creator, others, and ourselves.

In light of the aforementioned problems, I am calling Christian educators to encompass the creation story, the Great Commission, and divisions in the church, and in so doing, to focus on the function of spiritual gifts in the church to bridge the gaps over troubled waters. Methodologies, utilizing Christian education, are merely tools that are available to implement healing in the Christians' context. This healing will be offered to individuals as well as to leaders through self-help and interdependent assimilations as one makes a holistic connection with the love of God, through the church, and with people in the local community. Through Christian education, it is my desire that people will accept the possibilities of being liberated from negative traits and myths that have been perpetrated in history books, in many seminaries, churches,

---

[11]   Na'im Akbar, *Light from Ancient Africa* (Tallahassee, FL: Mind Production & Associates, 1994), 16.

and in stories that are passed down through the generations. It is also my desire that negated situations and negated mindsets be replaced with wholeness through God, Jesus Christ, and the Holy Spirit, educational methodologies, and other positive countermeasures.

> Black Sunday school classes are places where theological doctrines are taught, disputed, discussed, and clarified. Much of the theologizing takes its root in liberation because the concern is that Blacks come to understand ourselves from the belief or the concept that Blacks were sub-human beings. Blacks are seeking ways that will empower our ability to make sense out of the issues, beliefs, and challenges which confront us.[12]

> The Great Commission is affirmed by Sunday Schools in the Black church and most persons in this setting are willing to study and learn and process to tell and teach others. The aim becomes that of fulfilling the charge given, which instructs the followers of the way to teach newly made disciples along with older disciples (not in reference to age but to the length of time one has been involved in the Christian community), so that they are enabled and empowered to go and convince others likewise to become followers of the way. This brings in the dimension of evangelism because many who were unchurched have accepted the call after being led to Sunday School.[13]

> Black Sunday Schools need to place liberation and spiritual growth above all objectives. Yes, numerical growth is important, but our freedom and self-esteem are essential to our "being" and existence. If the church has to sacrifice liberation in order to grow numerically, them it might as well be dead. The goal of church growth and Sunday School growth in the black community is to foster change by helping blacks understand that the message of the Bible, indeed the message of Jesus,

---

[12] Mary A. Love, "Sunday School in the Black Community," in D. Campbell Wyckoff, ed., *Renewing the Sunday School and the CCD* (Birmingham, AL: Religious Education Press, 1986), 157.

[13] Ibid., 158.

is one of freedom and liberation. Without this general and comprehensive understanding there can be no real growth, no matter how large the number.[14]

In Christian education, individuals and leaders can study how biblical scriptures reveal Christ, giving Christians a helper to assist them in their plight. In the book of Acts we are told by Jesus, "But you will receive power when the Holy Spirit comes on you; and you will be my witnesses in Jerusalem, and in all Judea and Samaria, and to the ends of the earth."[15] This is in fact good news to all who are self-negated and who may feel in a helpless, isolated, and lonely condition of existence: Know that you are not alone. Jesus equipped his disciples with power to accomplish that which He commanded, and He gave his disciples a helper, the Holy Spirit, to assist them in staying spiritually connected. As He has done for his disciples, individuals He encountered and the families He touched, He will do the same for you and all believers.

Families are the moral fiber of our communities; nevertheless, our family value systems are decaying because many Africans in the Diaspora were encouraged to negate their heritage and/or replace it with a European or other value system. In past times, slaves were often separated from like-speaking slaves, in an effort to minimize the possibility of a revolt, and families were separated for financial reasons, causing disconnections among parents, children, and relatives. The intimate ties of a man to wife, mother to child, and brother to sister meant nothing to the oppressors, as each human head was slapped with a price. In this instance, they were alone and in many ways helpless; therefore, the family value system was severely damaged.[16] But as believers incorporate the mentality of connecting the entire village, lives and communities have been changed—and they will continue to be changed to positively reflect God's unselfish love.

In today's setting, as well as in the past, I must once again state the African proverb, "It takes a village to raise a child," because it was and is a vital link to the African Americans' and others' self-awareness and to the revitalization process that has assisted them in past and present times to

---

[14]   Harris, *Pastoral Theology*, 11-112.

[15]   Acts 1:8, NIV.

[16]   Charles Johnson and Patricia Smith, *Africans in America—America's Journey Through Slavery* (New York: Harcourt Brace, 1998), 273.

bridge the gap in America. The link to the African proverb will also enable individuals, leaders, and church members to continue press toward the mark of excellences within the walls of their homes, their churches, and their communities. We are all truly linked in oneness with God to be a part of His family, despite the quest of other nationalities to negate some who are, in many cases, people of color or of a different faith/religion practice.

So let individuals and leaders hear the stories of atrocities and injustices that have been placed on Africans, African Americans, and other people of color. Let them know the stories of cultural traumas in Africa, in America, in the West Indies, and in other locations worldwide. Let them listen intently to the stories of how many, by the grace of God, were able to pull themselves up, despite overwhelming hatred, injustice, discrimination, and many acts of violence perpetrated against people of color and impoverished people. With the assistance of their families, their communities, and their places of worship, many have beaten the odds and defeated negation and negative behavior traits. In many cases, because of effective leadership principles, faith practices, and holistic family systems, many have been strengthened to go on—despite feeling at times like a motherless child, or a man without a country.

Steps Toward a Personalized Theological Vision

1. *What destructive behavioral traits have you personally recognized in your community and/or in your church?*

2. *Theology is the study of God and the study of religion. Take some time to write a paragraph (or more) defining your personal theological belief.*

3. *How do you view God in your life, and what do you do to show your theological viewpoint?*

4. *What are your personal beliefs concerning liberation theology, social justice, and Blacks or African American theology?*

5.   *Theologically, how do we address those who are underserved and those who have been maltreated by society?*

6.   *Do you believe Jesus Christ is a liberator who addressed social justice in His ministry? Name ways social justice issues may be addressed in your context.*

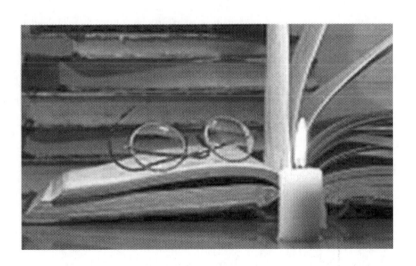

A Historical Perspective

This writing underscores how history has shown evidence of individuals, leaders, and, sometimes, family members associated with causing disconnected circumstances. At times our disconnections are created due to hatred, jealousy, wars, economic situations, and/or perceived and unperceived social conflicts and differences. Therefore, the following words are offered, which are written on the walls of two of the many slave castles scattered along the coast of West Africa:

> In everlasting memory of the anguish of our ancestors, may those who died rest in peace, may those who return find their roots, and may humanity never again perpetrate such injustice against humanity, we the Living Vow to Uphold This![17]

Along with this inscription one will find a sign affixed to the exit doors, which once led to waiting slave ships—a sign that reads, "The Door of No Return." The inscription displays historical evidence of an unjust and inhumane past, which helps one to understand the process of negation. I categorically declare that I believe this process was the physical attempt of some to enslave another human being physically and mentally. It is compounded by those who are not returning but who are staying disconnected from their heritage and not embracing those who were killed and erased from families in an attempt to control and treat others as mere commodities.

---

[17] *In Everlasting Memory.* An inscription on two slave castle courtyard entrance plaques located in Ghana, West Africa. Author unknown. Inscription not dated.

Due to horrific conditions, separations, and the maltreatment of Africans who were forced to endure unrest in the midst of their own countrymen, their villages, and aboard ship, for some, the search for one's roots still remains. It is here where many negative connotations were assimilated and it is here where one must begin the quest of understanding one's ancestral heritage and wholeness as God's disconnected people. It is also here from where one would travel westward to America, to the West Indies, eastward toward the inner territories of Africa, and northward to European countries to obtain further clarification concerning all the parties involved in such cruel injustices to humanity, as well as appreciating the strength of the survivors who were cast into slavery.

African spirits cannot and will not be relegated to the walls of these European slave castles where churches are placed in the midst of their courtyards. The bloodstained walls, floors, cells, and dungeons will not obscure the African spirits. Neither in the places where mutilated and decayed bodies of the strong-willed, who refused to submit, were left for days and sometimes weeks. These were places where the dead and the living were forced to occupy the same slave cell because their captors were too afraid of being overpowered and thus used this method as an opportunity to deter rebellion with inhumane psychological warfare-like strategies. Ancient African spirits will not be relegated to the many slave ships and plantations in an attempt to nullify the truth and negate rich African traditions, culture, and value systems that inspired greatness and the best from its people; a greatness that others desired and forcibly took in the name of slavery and as Christian missionaries.

In the book *African Cultural Values*, Kwame Gyekye writes, "When the European missionaries entered Africa to begin their religious work they found that they did not need to convert the African people to a belief in the existence of one God or in a life after death . . ."[18] Traditional African religion is said to be a natural religion and recognizes one supreme God, while some traditional African religions see God in everything: in the trees, in the mountains, in the sun, and in the moon.[19] Therefore, the practice of a monotheistic God was in Africa, and Africans served God in a communal venue within the confines of their villages.

---

[18] Gyekye Kwame, *African Cultural Values—An Introduction* (Lansing, MI: Sankofa, 1996), 4.

[19] Akbar, *Light*, 19.

Historically, negative traits were seen by many Europeans as they asserted not only their faith practices on Africans in the United States, but also their beliefs concerning solutions to what they alleged to be problems with Africans. In fact, in 1712, a man by the name of Willie Lynch articulated this very sentiment when he wrote in his letter, "I am here to help you solve some of your problems with slaves . . . They must love, respect, and trust only us . . . (this practice) if used intensely for one year, the slaves themselves will remain perpetually distrustful of each other."[20]

Some have negated the validity of Willie Lynch and his speech because there was no other written documentation produced by him on file. Nevertheless, whoever devised this psychological tactic has in many instances caused Africans in the Diaspora to negate themselves as well as others. This negation has continued for almost three hundred years.

In a lecture by Anthony Elmore Sr., he quotes Dr. John Clark, who wrote, "The events which transpired five thousand years ago, five years ago or five minutes ago, have determined what will happen five minutes from now, five years from now or five thousand years from now. All history is a current event." [21] If Dr. Clark's assessments are correct, therefore, African Americans need only to search their theological and physical history to conclude that they indeed, "are *more than conquerors through Him that loved us.*"[22] God created humanity in His image and in His likeness[23]; consequently the fact remains that, in spite of being negated, raped, and killed by others, Africans, African Americans, and people of color are all truly more than conquerors!

During a spiritual and theological journey to Ghana, West Africa, this writer became invested in connecting others to Africa and to the people who reside there. It was the sight of the slave castles, as well as the festive and Spirit-filled experiences in the local churches that captivated my inner spirit. These encounters, along with the Ghanaian people, have mesmerized me and left a positive impact upon my soul; yet they were more like visions that cried out to me, as I plan to continue to embrace the festive spirits of my ancestral ties into ministry, through Christian education and

---

[20] Willie Lynch's Speech on His Methods for Controlling Slaves.

[21] Anthony Amp, *A Buddhist Lecture on Willie Lynch's Speech on His Methods for Controlling Slaves.*

[22] Romans 8:37b.

[23] Genesis 1:26, 27.

evangelism. Also, I have been compelled to honor my ancestors and those who overcame adversity, as well as those who were shunned and negated because of their heritage. Therefore, through self-help, interdependence, and Christian education, I pray that leaders and the laity of churches will actively become involved in church missions so that they too will be able to likewise embrace this quest.

The quest of embracing one's heritage provides an additional framework for this writing because it takes leaders and the laity from self-negation to self-help and then to independence.[24] It reaches out to negated souls in their condition of existence to assist in their spiritual (theological) and physical (hereditary) wholeness. It also serves to integrate the message of being helped and helping others to achieve a holistic ministry as a servant of God while realizing one's African/ethnic connection amidst one's spiritual gift(s) and how they function with others in the body of Christ.

Steps Toward Personalizing Your Historical Perspective

1. *What are some historical stories (written and verbal) that may have caused disconnected circumstances in your life, in your environment, and within your and other ethnicities?*

2. *How can your stories help reverse disconnected circumstances in your life?*

3. *Do you believe you have disconnected yourself from your heritage and from the country/continent of your ancestors? Why or why not?*

4. *Have you or someone in your family completed an ancestry tree? Why or why not?*

5. *Have you traced your ancestors back to Africa or another continent, and have you visited the birthplace of your ancestors? Why or why not?*

---

[24] Ralph Reavis, *Apostles of Self-Help and Independence* (African-American Publishers of Virginia, LLC, 1999).

6. *Have you been on a evangelistic or missionary trip or help someone else to go on a mission trips?*

7. *God created humanity in His image and in His likeness. Some historical stories have placed African American beginnings amidst slave ships and plantations. How can you use and teach others about the strength it took your ancestors to overcome overt psychological trauma to help you become more than a conqueror in Christ Jesus?*

8. *Do you believe it is important to embrace your heritage? Why or why not?*

9. *What steps can you take to begin embracing your African heritage as well as your African American heritage?*

Psychological and Sociological Considerations

Biblical psychology and sociology are extremely complex, but this writing seeks to underscore their relevance to the reader's condition of existence. It is written that Africans were stripped of their dignity and marched naked through the rough terrain of Africa (and across America), to inhumane slave castles, through treacherous waters, to appalling slave markets, and then forced to work in environments where they were prohibited from speaking in their native tongues.[25] The writer asserts that this was a part of the psychological warfare perpetrated in slavery, and in many ways, was a plan devised to negate Africans as human beings. The Africans who were enslaved were not treated as human beings, but as commodities, thus they were negated as humans from the very beginning of their exploitation.[26] Then those who survived such horrendous maltreatment were also separated from their families, from like-speaking Africans, as well as from their social continent. "Psychological trauma also occurred when children witnessed the daily humiliation of their parents and other African Americans at the hands of European Americans, regardless of whether they themselves had been slaves or had knowledge or feelings for Africa." [27]

---

[25] Charles Johnson, WGBH Series Research Team, *Africans in America—America's Journey Through Slavery*, (WGBH Boston Video, 1998), DVD.

[26] Alton Hornsby Jr., "African Americans," *World Book Online Reference Centre*, http://www.worldbookonline.com/ar?/na/ar/co/ar006745.htm, November 16, 2003.

[27] Ron Eyerman, *Cultural Trauma: Slavery and Formation of African Americans Identity* (New York: Cambridge University Press, 2001), 2-5,

The previous statements were examples of the beginning process of enslavement (prisoners of war), as well as the psychological warfare tactics that integrated sociological implications. While it is written that European nations began the slave trade, because Western Africans were brought to European colonies in the United States, it must also be written that Europeans were sometimes assisted by Africans who were often instrumental in the beginning phases of these warfare tactics and trauma. Nevertheless, another type of traumatic experience suffered is the cultural trauma that "refers to a dramatic loss of identity and meaning, a tear in the social fabric . . ."[28]

A "tear in the social fabric" has caused not only a traumatic experience, but at times it has also caused a division in African American churches and in their communities. In the book, *Blowing the Trumpet in Open Court*, Dr. Boykin Sanders states that a social tear (colonialism) has also occurred in Africa: "It de-Africanized Africa."[29] This tear in the social fabric is the summation of some gravitating toward Africa, some toward Europe, while others are gravitating or torn somewhere among other ethnicities. Regardless of which piece of social fabric one rests upon, or has infiltrated, our individual placement or displacement affects individuals, churches, and community involvement. African Americans were often publicly praised if they were successful in society, and criticized if their behavior was what European societies deemed unsuccessful or unacceptable. This, in essence, is the meaning of cultural trauma, which "refers to a dramatic loss of identity and meaning; a tear in the social fabric."[30] This affects the social standard of one's perspective and behavior in the church and in the community.

As individuals and leaders reflect on their societal standing, I would like to offer the Holy Bible as the most authoritative text on the subject of human behavior. In the Bible, one may examine human behavior since creation, and thereby seek remedies as one delves into what is called biblical psychology. Biblical psychology addresses God's (the Creator) relationship to mankind, and the behaviors and social conditions that existed when man was separated and subjugated to physical, spiritual, and

---

28 Eyerman, *Cultural Trauma*, 2.
29 Boykin Sanders *Blowing the Trumpet in Open Court—Prophetic Judgment and Liberation*, 108.
30 Eyerman, *Cultural Trauma*, 2.

mental enslavement. It is through the word of God that one will be able to see one's negativity (sin), which is the underlying problem that exists and has existed for thousands of years. Individuals and leaders should realize that godly remedies are the solution to spiritual wounds one acquires through any type of imprisonment (enslavement, self-negated or inflicted by another) and while they are on the battlefield of the Lord.

Too many brothers and sisters are ashamed of parts of their history, such as tribal wars, being sold as commodities, forced voyages to America, and imprisonment (enslavement). In essence, they have been told or taught to be ashamed of their skin color. Others have attempted to assimilate features of their subjugators, while some have dyed their hair blonde and/or used blue contact lenses to change the color of their eyes; others have had operations to alter their prominent facial features. Some have intentionally moved into European neighborhoods to say that "they have arrived," even when they have fought their neighbors to move and remain in some neighborhoods. Some are in many ways sending mixed signals—psychological and sociological signals—to their children and to younger generations by negating themselves and assimilating other ethnic identities. Nevertheless, it must be stated that decisions to make these assimilations are sometimes due to inequalities that exist throughout America and throughout the world. Blatant inequalities in America have caused some Americans to assume European-American cultural and behavioral practices in an effort to seek better education, to acquire better housing, and to assume a perceived higher social standing in the eyes of others. In other words, some are attempting to get their fair share of the American pie, and/or fit into the norms of society by becoming Europeanized.

Therefore, if individuals, leaders, and Christian educators are going to revalidate, reeducate, and reclaim their heritage, and become connected with other believers, they must begin by reversing the psychological and sociological damage of negativity of all involved persons in their church and in society as a whole—blacks, whites, yellows, pinks, and reds. Individuals and Christian leaders from all ethnicities must stand up against self-negation and damaging situations! African Americans should say from the depths of their inner spirit, "I am somebody. I have a rich, noble, and proud heritage; however exploited and however pained my history has been, I'm black, but *I'm black and beautiful*" (Lischer, 1995,

101)."[31] People of all ethnicities, of all cultures, creed, and color must realize that we who are believers are more than conquerors in Christ Jesus. We were created in the image of the Almighty God, the Creator of this universe.

Steps Toward Understanding Tears in Social Fabrics

1. *What is your understanding of biblical psychology and biblical sociology, and how do they affect you and your environment?*

2. *Do you believe a "tear in the social fabric" (a dramatic loss of identity and meaning) has caused separations in your life or made you feel like a "motherless child"?*

3. *Explain some divisions in your life and steps you have taken or can take to mend the tears in your social fabric.*

4. *Today many children are subjected to psychological trauma. How can you and your local church/community leaders address psychological trauma in your community?*

5. *What steps can you take to reverse psychological trauma within you?*

6. *How you use the Holy Bible as the most authoritative text to assist you in eradicating negative behavioral traits and reverse psychological trauma?*

7. *What steps are you willing to take to revalidate, reeducate, and reclaim who you are and why God created you? And, are you willing to teach others?*

---

[31]   Eyerman, *Cultural Trauma*, (New York: Cambridge University Press). 210.

Biblical Considerations

"He will speak peace to His people, to His faithful, to those who
turn to Him in their hearts. Surely His salvation is at hand for
those who fear Him."[32]

Biblically, the scriptures reveal how humanity was created in God's image.[33] The Holy Bible tells the story of one's initial spiritual foundation and connection to God. It also unveils the importance of reestablishing one's physical connection. In fact, the importance of one's lineage is highlighted throughout the Biblical scriptures. One can begin to understand who he or she is through the understanding of one's physical and spiritual heritage, which is not completed until the disconnected links are re-attached through the body of Christ. It is the Universal Architect who established a solid foundation for *obedient and faithful* Christians to build upon. This asserts that one's foundation is relevant in one's walk through life. If one fails to learn from one's history, one is doomed to repeat and/or pass on negative behavior traits that could have been avoided in life. Additionally, in order to learn from one's history one must identify, study, and be acquainted with it.

It is not enough to only accept God as one's Creator. One must also be grounded in God's foundation. The evidence of one's faithfulness is further revealed in the expression of the good fruit one bears in life.

16 You will know them by their fruits. Are grapes gathered
from thorns, or figs from thistles? 17 In the same way, every

---

[32] Psalm 85:8b-9a, NRSV.

[33] Genesis 1:26.

good tree bears good fruit, but the bad tree bears bad fruit. 18 A good tree cannot bear bad fruit, nor can a bad tree bear good fruit. 19 Every tree that does not bear good fruit is cut down and thrown into the fire. 20 Thus you will know them by their fruits. [34]

In essence, God's salvation plan reestablishes humanity; Luke wrote that "all flesh shall see the salvation of God,"[35] and the Psalmist inscribed, "He will speak peace to His people, to His faithful, to those who turn to Him in their hearts. Surely His salvation is at hand for those who fear Him."[36] Nevertheless, the connection toward one's lineage is vital to understanding and not repeating past negative events.

It is in the beginning, through God's foundational plan, that humanity was given dominion over nonhumans. Man was told to subdue the earth, not the people of the earth. In the book of Genesis there was neither physical separation nor self-negation in the beginning when God created the world. Then God said,

> "Let us make man in our image, in our likeness, and let them rule over the fish of the sea and the birds of the air, over the livestock, over all the creatures that move along the ground." So God created man in His own image, in the image of God, He created him; male and female He created them. God blessed them and said to them, "Be fruitful and increase in number: fill the earth and subdue it. Rule over the fish of the sea and the birds of the air and over every living creature that moves on the ground."[37]

Also, God's foundational plans were further amplified through the writings of Paul as Paul penned:

> 10 According to the grace of God given to me, like a skilled master builder I laid a foundation, and someone else is building

---

[34] Matthews 7:16-20, NRSV.

[35] Luke 3:6.

[36] Psalms 85:8b-9a, NRSV.

[37] Genesis 1:26-28, NIV.

on it. Each builder must choose with care how to build on it. 11 For no one can lay any foundation other than the one that has been laid; that foundation is Jesus Christ. 12 Now if anyone builds on the foundation with gold, silver, precious stones, wood, hay, straw—13 the work of each builder will become visible, for the Day will disclose it, because it will be revealed with fire, and the fire will test what sort of work each has done. 14 If what has been built on the foundation survives, the builder will receive a reward. 15 If the work is burned up, the builder will suffer loss; the builder will be saved, but only as through fire. 16 Do you not know that you are God's temple and that God's Spirit dwells in you? 17 If anyone destroys God's temple, God will destroy that person. For God's temple is holy, and you are that temple. [38]

It is God's people who are separated from the world, but it is God who is exalted above all. In the body of Christ, men and women have been given positions. In the scriptures, it was man who decided that he should be elevated above another, build his own foundation by his negative outpouring—and such is the case in the story of Cain and Abel.[39]

Also, in the book of Exodus, the Egyptians negated one nationality in order to effectively elevate themselves.

8 Now a new king arose over Egypt, who did not know Joseph. 9 He said to his people, "Look, the Israelite people are more numerous and more powerful than we. 10 Come, let us deal shrewdly with them, or they will increase and, in the event of war, join our enemies and fight against us and escape from the land." 11 Therefore they set taskmasters over them to oppress them with forced labor. They built supply cities, Pithom and Rameses, for Pharaoh. 12 But the more they were oppressed, the more they multiplied and spread, so that the Egyptians came to dread the Israelites. 13 The Egyptians became ruthless in imposing tasks on the Israelites, 14 and made their lives bitter with hard service in mortar and brick and in every kind of field

---

[38]   I Corinthians 3: 10-16, NRSV.

[39]   Genesis 4:7, KJV.

labor. They were ruthless in all the tasks that they imposed on them.[40]

Throughout biblical writings, we find God's people being separated and mistreated. In the book of Exodus we discover Moses telling Pharaoh several times to "let my people [God's people] go."[41] All across the world, and possibly in your home and in your community, souls are still crying out, *Let my people go!*

Despite man's quest to negate and mistreat some for superiority and division, a divine call was mandated to make disciples in all nations baptize and teach other God's foundation plans through the biblical teachings of Christ Jesus.

> 19 "Go therefore and make disciples of all nations, baptizing them in the name of the Father and of the Son and of the Holy Spirit, 20 and teaching them to obey everything that I have commanded you. And remember, I am with you always, to the end of the age." [42]

It is in these scriptures that the writer finds the mandate to spread God's word to others, and in effect, the process is repeated as new learners are trained (becoming disciples of Jesus Christ) and the Word of God is taught throughout all nations. Nevertheless, one must first learn God's foundational plan through the teachings of Jesus Christ. As one becomes an effective disciple (student), then one will spread the good news of Jesus Christ. This process would be reproduced until the gospel is spread throughout all nations. Each one should teach one.

As one becomes an effective student of the Bible, one begins to recognize self-negation traits in order to address and effectively change one's behavior, as Peter recognized when he denied Jesus and remembered that which was spoken to him concerning denying the Christ.

> "the bystanders, "This man is one of them." 70 But again he denied it. Then after a little while the bystanders again said to

---

[40]   Exodus 1:8-14, NRSV.

[41]   Exodus 8-10, NKJV.

[42]   Matthew 28: 18-20, RSV.

Peter, "Certainly you are one of them; for you are a Galilean." 71 But he began to curse, and he swore an oath, "I do not know this man you are talking about." 72 At that moment the cock crowed for the second time. Then Peter remembered that Jesus had said to him, "Before the cock crows twice, you will deny me three times." And he broke down and wept.[43]

Negative behavior traits are often repeated until one comes to the knowledge and understanding of Christianity and who one is in Christ. Christians belong to God and are offered wholeness in the body of Christ. It is self-negated behavioral traits that cause defeat in one's life; when repentance is asked and sins are forgiven, wholeness in a believer's life is restored. Through Christian education, and by receiving God the Father, His son Jesus Christ, and the Holy Spirit as the Comforter, [44] one will receive power to witness to all nations. This writer believes the gospel must be preached to the disenfranchised, and God is calling His leaders to proclaim this message to all males and females alike around the world.

18"The Spirit of the Lord *is* upon me, because he hath anointed me to preach the gospel to the poor; he hath sent me to heal the brokenhearted, to preach deliverance to the captives, and recovering of sight to the blind, to set at liberty them that are bruised, 19 to preach the acceptable year of the Lord."[45]

In building upon a solid foundation and getting connected through effective Christian leadership training, the individual and spiritual leaders are educated through Christian education and biblical transformative methodologies. Individuals and leaders should address a more excellent way toward wholeness by knowing whose body they are representing through their spiritual and physical lineage. They should first embrace those who are in the body of Christ (Genesis 1:26-27 and 2 Corinthians 5:17-21). Individuals and leaders should be equipped to delve within their spiritual gifts and embrace their functions as members in the body.

---

[43] Mark 14:72, NKJV.

[44] Acts 1:8, NIV.

[45] Luke 4:18-19 KJV.

4 Now there are varieties of gifts, but the same Spirit; 5 and there are varieties of services, but the same Lord; 6 and there are varieties of activities, but it is the same God who activates all of them in everyone. 7 To each is given the manifestation of the Spirit for the common good.[46]

Christians will understand and begin to work with other members, complementing their spiritual gifts and the ministries they have been given by the Holy Spirit and assigned in the body of Christ.

14 Indeed, the body does not consist of one member but of many. 15 If the foot would say, "Because I am not a hand, I do not belong to the body," that would not make it any less a part of the body. 16 And if the ear would say, "Because I am not an eye, I do not belong to the body," that would not make it any less a part of the body. 17 If the whole body were an eye, where would the hearing be? If the whole body were hearing, where would the sense of smell be? 18 But as it is, God arranged the members in the body, each one of them, as he chose. 19 If all were a single member, where would the body be? 20 As it is, there are many members, yet one body. 21 The eye cannot say to the hand, "I have no need of you," nor again the head to the feet, "I have no need of you." 22 On the contrary, the members of the body that seem to be weaker are indispensable, 23 and those members of the body that we think less honorable we clothe with greater honor, and our less respectable members are treated with greater respect; 24 whereas our more respectable members do not need this. But God has so arranged the body, giving the greater honor to the inferior member, 25 that there may be no dissension within the body, but the members may have the same care for one another. 26 If one member suffers, all suffer together with it; if one member is honored, all rejoice together with it.[47]

---

[46] I Corinthians 12: 4-7, NRSV.
[47] I Corinthians 12: 14-26, NRSV.

Individuals and leaders must be taught the importance of how to suffer and rejoice daily as one body in Christ (I Corinthians 12:26) so that a more excellent way may be revealed through love as the writer of Corinthians says, "strive for the greater gifts. And I will show you a still more excellent way."[48]

Steps Toward Greatness

1. *Write down spiritual/biblical texts that inspire you and read or recite (aloud) your list at least three times daily.*

2. *Get involved in a proactive and effective Christian education teaching program. Use seminary trained Christian educators, if possible.*

---

[48]   I Corinthian 12:31.

Let's Get Connected

"United We Stand and Divided We Shall Surely Fall"

We are connected and disconnected in life because of similarities and differences. We are connected by family, faith, denomination, love, languages, education, birth, fraternities, sororities, memberships, political parties, skin color, hatred, national disasters, or a host of other commonalities. One may say that circumstances or commonalities can connect one to another, or dangerous and daunting indifferences and self-inflicted experiences can widen the gap of disconnection. Family, faith, love, and general commonalities may seem like natural circumstances that bring or keep some people connected. Major tragedies, world wars, terrorist attacks, devastating disasters, major oil spills, the death of a terrorist leader or a family member also evoke passion, a sense of stillness and discomfort, which may connect and bring others together. Still yet, some are only linked for a given period of time or until the tragedy or disaster is adverted or the person has moved on to another event in their life. National disasters like a tsunami, a hurricane, a tornado, an earthquake, or an attack of war or terrorism, connect people from around the world to assist others who are in a calamitous predicament and in need of assistance.

During hurricane Katrina, the **American Red Cross** utilized more than 244,000 relief workers for its hurricane response efforts, helped more than 1.4 million families (more than four million people) with direct emergency assistance, served more than 68 million meals and snacks, provided more than 3.8 million overnight stays in more than 1,400 shelters, distributed more than 540,000 comfort kits and clean up kits, and made almost 597,000 health services contacts and more than 826,000 mental health services contacts.[49] During World War II, volunteers staffed millions of jobs in community service roles, such as the USO and Red Cross. After terrorists invaded and attacked the United States, volunteers worked tireless hours helping others they did not know.[50] As the National Health Care Reform bill was introduced in the United States, many aligned on one side or the other side; some were for the bill, some were against the bill, and others were somewhere in between.[51]

People around the world are connected, and if we are to survive and come together as families, communities, cities, countries, or continents, it is imperative that we seek ways of connecting to others without waiting on a major catastrophe to dismantle our egos and pride. Ask yourself, Shall I wait on a major event before I am connected and offer assistance to help others? If I know a large pothole is in the road, and a person is heading in the direction of the pothole, do I wait for them to fall into it before going to their rescue, or do I seek to connect with that person and help them when I see their direction of travel? Furthermore, how do I get along in communities where diverse faith organizations practice serving a loving and kind God, but they seldom cross denominational lines and they oppose those who do not look like them, believe what they believe, or worship the way they worship? In the same breath, how do government officials find connections to accomplish the greater good for all people whom they vowed to serve? Lastly, how do elected officials not accomplish this task, without some type of mutiny or treason against him or her who has been elected, called, and confirmed as the president, king, queen or czar of their particular country?

It is written, "United we stand and divided we fall,"[52] but do we believe in these seven simple yet complex words without prejudice? Seven words that make up one statement, which removes narrow-mindedness from

---

49 http://www.dhs.gov/xfoia/archives/gc_1157649340100.shtm

50 http://en.wikipedia.org/wiki/September_11_attacks

51 http://www.healthreform.gov

52 The phrase has been attributed to Aesop, both directly in his fable *The Four Oxen and the Lion*[1] and indirectly from *The Bundle of Sticks*[2]. The first attributed use in modern times is to John Dickinson in his revolutionary war song The Liberty Song. In the song, first published in the Boston Gazette in July 1768, he wrote: "Then join hand in hand, brave Americans all! By uniting we stand, by dividing we fall!" http://en.wikipedia.org/wiki/United_we_stand,_divided_we_fall

the rearview mirror and places connection in the forefront of the art of connectivity. It is said that Sunday worship (11:00 AM hour) time is the most segregated time in America. Have we become so content at being or becoming many islands of one? Are we content with living in a world where we often quiver and say, *Where can I go?, What must I do?*, and, *I certainly did it my way?* In the end, are we to say *Who must I negate?, What must I conquer?, Where must I go?*, and, *Must I do it alone?* To get to where I am self-centered and self-productive, utilizing my individual ideology and worldly pride? I pray the answer will always be no. Please stay positive, stay connected and be true to thy own self!

Steps Toward Getting Connected

1. *Name those who have been disconnected from your life.*

2. *What steps have you taken or what step do you need to take to mend disconnected ties you have caused or another has caused?*

3. *What has caused you to disconnect yourself from others?*

4. *How can you help others to seek positive connections in their lives?*

5. *How can you create space and theological conversations for people of diverse faith practices with others who have disconnected themselves?*

APPENDIX A

The Black Family Pledge

by Dr. Maya Angelou

BECAUSE we have forgotten our ancestors,
Our children no longer give honor.

BECAUSE we have lost the path our ancestors cleared
Kneeling in perilous undergrowth,
Our children cannot find their way.

BECAUSE we have banished the God of our ancestor,
Our children cannot pray.

BECAUSE the old wails of our ancestors have faded beyond our hearing,
Our children cannot hear us crying.

BECAUSE we have abandoned our wisdom of mothering and fathering,
Our befuddled children give birth to children
They neither want nor understand.

BECAUSE we have forgotten how to love, the adversary is within our
gates and holds us up to the mirror of the world shouting,
"Regard the loveless."

Therefore we pledge to bind ourselves to one another, to embrace our lowliest, to keep company with our loneliest, to educate our illiterate, to feed our starving, to clothe our ragged, to do all good things, Knowing that we are more than keepers of our brothers and sisters.

We are our brothers and sisters.[53]

---

[53] Maya Angelou, *The Black Family Pledge*.

APPENDIX B

Willie Lynch's Speech on His Methods for Controlling Slaves

"I have a fool proof method for controlling *(negating)* Black Slaves. I guarantee every one of you that if installed correctly, it will control the slaves for at least 300 years. My method is simple and members of your family and any Overseer can use it.

I have outlined a number of difference(s) among the slaves; and I take these differences and make them bigger. I use fear, distrust, and envy for control purposes. These methods have worked on my modest plantation in the West Indies and [they] will work throughout the South. Take this simple little list of differences, think about them. On top of my list is "Age" but it is there only because it begins with an "A." The second is "Color" or "Shade," there is intelligence, size, sex, size of plantation, status of plantation, attitude of owner, whether the slaves live in the valley, on a hill, East, West, North, or South, have a fine or coarse hair, or is tall or short. Now that you have a list of differences, I shall give you an outline of action but before that, I shall assure you that distrust is stronger than trust and envy is stronger than adulation, respect, and admiration.

The Black Slave, after receiving this indoctrination, shall carry on and will become self-refueling and self-generating for hundreds of years, maybe thousands.

Don't forget you must pitch the old black versus the young black and the young black male against the old black male. You must use the dark skin slave vs. the light skin slave and the light skin slaves vs. the dark skin slaves. You must also have your white servants and overseers distrust all blacks, but it is necessary that your slaves trust and depend on us. They must love, respect, and trust only us.

Gentlemen, these Kits are keys to control, use them. Have your wives and children use them, never miss an opportunity. My plan is guaranteed and the good thing about this plan is that if used intensely for one year the slaves themselves will remain perpetually distrustful."[54]

---

[54]   Willie Lynch's Speech, His Methods of Controlling Slaves.

APPENDIX C

THE TIMELINE

TIME LINE CHART

The Art of Connectivity: A Call for Unity Within A Diverse Society

Week One	Week Two	Week Three	Week Four	Week Five	Week Six
Facilitator Rev. Dr Change Lesson One	*Facilitator* Rev. Dr Change Lesson Two	*Facilitator* Rev. Dr Change Lesson Three	*Facilitator* Rev. Dr Change Lesson Four	*Facilitator* Rev. Dr Change Lesson Five	*Facilitator* Rev. Dr Change Lesson Six
Introduction *(Pretest)* Getting Connected: - The Self-Negated Person and Steps Employed to Connect Individuals, leaders, those in ministry, and the laity	Setting the Captives Free - Who I am and where is God amidst Tragedy and Chaos And Troubled Waters - Separation and God's Healing Spirit	Christian Education - Seeking Enrichment, Encirclement and Empowerment through Enlightenment	Where do we go from Here? - Social Consciousness for the 21st Century and Beyond	Putting it all Together - Discipleship and the Importance of Staying Connected Empowering the Leadership Summary *(Post Test)*	United We Stand and Divided We Shall Surely Fall - Dinner / Guest Speaker Presentation of Certificates
Location: TBA	Location: TBA	Location: TBA	Location: TBA	Location: TBA	Location: TBA
Time: 7:00 to 8:50 p.m.	Time: 7:00 to 8:50 p.m.	Time: 7:00 to 8:50 p.m.	Time: 7:00 to 8:50 p.m.	Time: 7:00 to 8:50 p.m.	Time: 7:00 to 8:50 p.m.

APPENDIX D

THE LESSON PLANS

Getting Connected

The Self-Negated Person and Steps Employed to Connect Leaders, Those in Ministry, and the Laity

Main Idea

The main idea of this lesson is to teach a more excellent way of effectively connecting leadership, ministries, and the laity, through biblical transformation and transformative methodologies. Learners will discuss negative attitudes, behavior traits and traditions that lead one away from the church and toward destructive courses of self-negation. This session will assist the learners in seeing positive and effective connections associated within this context. The problem areas of this project are a disconnected body of believers (leaders and laity); disconnected lines of communication; ineffective ministries; ineffective Christian education training; leaders and laity who are not developed (enriched), not empowered, and not embracing self and others; disconnected heritage (or a negative association with one's heritage); and disconnection associated with leaders, ministries, and the laity not functioning according to biblical principles and the church's mission statement. Christian educators, evangelists, preachers, leaders, those in ministry, and the laity must refocus their teaching strategies/ methodologies for learners of all ages to assist believers as well as for unbelievers to see the importance of Christian education in their lives.

The Goal

The goal of this session is to stimulate and facilitate leaders, those in ministry, and the laity to make a positive connection to God within oneself, the local church, and the one's community while focusing on a more excellent way of connecting. Lastly, learners/participants will be taught the importance of getting and staying connected while waiting on the spiritual gift(s) allocated by the Holy Spirit for enrichment, empowerment, and encirclement, amid self-help and interdependence methodologies.

Instructional Objectives

Upon completion of this lesson, the learners should be able to:

1. Participate in and complete a pretest.

2. Summarize verbally your interpretation of negative attitudes and behavior traits.

3. Describe at least one course of self-negation that leads leaders and/or laity to disconnect oneself, one's heritage, and one's faith practices, thereby assuming and embracing the characteristics of others' nations from previous readings, biblical stories, or this session.

4. Discuss aspects of cultural trauma in the church and in the local and global communities.

5. State in their own words the importance of positive connections between the leaders, those in ministry, and the laity.

Time	Teaching Activities	Resources
	The lesson opens with scripture and prayer, which will focus on waiting on the Holy Spirit for spiritual empowerment, encirclement, and enrichment, amid self-help and interdependence methodologies.	Podium, tables, chairs, and the Holy Bible
	(The classroom(s) has been set up to facilitate class participation.)	Classroom(s) and materials are set up in advance
	Reading of the lesson objectives and goals	Objectives and goals
	A pretest will be administered	The Pretest
	An overview of the lesson will be given along with a handout on terminologies.	Lesson overview / terminology handouts
	The facilitator will shows selected scenes from the video Africans in America: America's Journey through Slavery, or a similar video to facilitate discussion during the session.	Television, DVD player Cart and extension cord

Setting the Captives Free

Who I Am and Where is God Amidst Tragedy and Chaos
Spiritual and Physical Disconnections and God's Healing Spirit

Main Idea

The main idea of this lesson is to teach and introduce leaders, those in ministry, and the laity transformative methodologies of biblical psychology and sociology. Learner will delve into ways of being set free through God's healing spirit, spiritual gifts, and self-help and interdependence methodologies.

The Goal

The goal of this teaching session is to stimulate and facilitate those who desire to make a connection to God, within oneself, the local church, and one's community. This session will focus on I Corinthians 12:26 to facilitate discussions on knowing how to suffer and rejoice as one body in Christ.

Instructional Objectives

Upon completion of this lesson, the learners should be able to:

1. Discuss aspects of liberation theology, biblical psychology, sociology, and W. E. B. Du Bois theory.
2. Verbally describe the impact of Willie Lynch's Speech and other psychological tactics employed.
3. Discuss at least one positive (spiritual) approach of suffering and rejoicing as one body in Christ.

Time		Teaching Activities	Resources
Opening **05 minutes**		The lesson opens with scripture and prayer that will focus on the positive aspects of biblical psychology and sociology while getting and staying connected to God. (The classroom(s) has been set up to facilitate class participation).	Podium, tables, chairs, and the Holy Bible Classroom(s) and materials are set up in advance Lesson objectives and goals
Presenting the **Subject** **20 minutes**		Reading of the lesson objectives and goals An overview of the lesson will be given along with a handout on terminologies.	Overview
		The facilitator will show selected scenes from the DVD Africans in America: America's Journey through Slavery to facilitate discussion during the session.	Terminologies handouts Television, DVD player Cart and extension cord
Exploring the **Subject** **45 minutes**		Lecture and discussions: • Liberation theology • Biblical psychology	Tables, chairs, a podium, a laptop computer, and the LCD machine Notebook, papers, and pens

Time	Teaching Activities	Resources
	• Biblical sociology in W.E. B. Du Bois theory • "African Freedom and Liberation in American" • The impact of Willie Lynch's Speech and other psychological tactics employed • Aspects of troubled waters in America • Bridging troubled waters (justice through reconciliation) • Positive aspects of setting the captives free	
Concluding the Session 20 minutes	An overview (recap) of today's lesson and special emphasis on empowerment and upcoming sessions. Learners' question and answer session. Christian education classroom(s) at your church	Tables, chairs, podium, a laptop computer, and the LCD machine Notebook, papers, and pens

Time	Teaching Activities	Resources
	The students are members of your church, and learners, preachers, teachers, and parishioners from local churches and members of the community	Classroom(s)
Setting	* This lesson is designed to be taught during a mid-week Bible study class, a retreat, vacation Bible classes, or during Sunday morning church school with special emphasis (or a weekly theme) on getting connected through empowerment, encirclement, enrichment, self-help, and interdependence methodologies.	
Students **Notes**	* Participants will receive a certificate of completion at the end of the training session if 80 percent of the classes are attended, active participation is demonstrated, and lesson objectives are met.	

Time	Teaching Activities	Resources
	* Training sessions are lineal, therefore learners are encouraged to attend all sessions to maximize their learning effectiveness.	Classroom(s)
	* To stimulate the learning process in the classroom(s), open-ended questions will be used throughout the sessions.	
Discussion Questions	1. How do you envision the following subjects making a positive impact in your life, upon those in ministry, and others in your context: ✓ Liberation theology ✓ Biblical psychology ✓ Biblical sociology	

Time	Teaching Activities	Resources
	2. What psychological impact of Willie Lynch's Speech (if any) do you believe is relevant to you and other members of your church and your community?	
	3. What positive countermeasures are available to begin bridging troubled waters in your life?	
	4. How can you assist others in bridging troubled waters?	
	5. How many additional positive countermeasures can we come up with as a class to present to the leaders in the church?	

Christian Education

Seeking Enrichment, Encirclement, and Empowerment Through Enlightenment

Main Idea

The main idea of this lesson is to teach leaders, those in ministry, and the laity transformative methodologies through Christian education that will serve as vehicles that one would navigate to embrace positive changes in a holistic body. In effect, this project will teach a more excellent way of effectively connecting leadership, ministries, and the laity, by seeking positive enrichment (development), encirclement (surrounding), and empowerment (authorization) through biblical enlightenment (clarification).

The Goal

The goal of this teaching session is to stimulate those who desire to make positive connections through Christian education. This teaching session will employ Christian education methodologies as vehicles of transformation that one may use to effectively navigate toward enlightenment. Learners will be taught the importance of waiting on the Holy Spirit for spiritual enrichment, empowerment, and encirclement, amid self-help and interdependence methodologies.

Instructional Objectives

Upon completion of this lesson, the learners should be able to:

1. Describe the importance of effective Christian education in ministry as well as in one's personal life.

2. Verbally discuss encirclement and empowerment in your context.

3. Verbally name at least one positive aspect of self-help and interdependence methodologies through Christian education.

Time	Teaching Activities	Resources
Opening **05 minutes**	The lesson opens with scripture and prayer, which will focus on seeking Christian education for spiritual empowerment, encirclement, and enrichment, amid self-help and interdependence methodologies.	Podium, tables, chairs, and the Holy Bible
Presenting **the Subject** **20 minutes**	(The classroom(s) has been set up for class participation.) Opening remarks and an overview.	Classroom(s) and materials are set up in advance Television, DVD player Television/DVD cart Extension cord
Exploring **the Subject** **45 minutes**	The facilitator will show selected scenes from the DVD Africans in America: America's Journey through Slavery, to facilitate discussion during the session. Lecture and discussions: • Understanding enrichment, encirclement, and empowerment through enlightenment (transformative measures) in the learners' context.	Tables, chairs, podium, laptop computer, and the LCD machine Notebook, papers, and pens

Time	Teaching Activities	Resources
	• Building a faith community that encourages and empowers leaders and the laity to grow spiritually and to work harmoniously utilizing Christian education approaches. • Understanding different approaches in Christian education (transformative, religious education, spiritual development, and the faith community).[1]	
Concluding the Session 20 minutes	An overview (recap) of today's lesson and special emphasis on empowerment and upcoming sessions. Learners' question and answer session.	Tables, chairs, podium, laptop computer, and the LCD machine.
Setting	Christian education classroom(s) at your church.	Classroom(s)
Students	The students are members of your church, and learners, preachers, teachers, and parishioners from local churches, and members of the community.	

Time	Teaching Activities	Resources
Notes:	* This lesson is designed to be taught during; a mid-week bible study class, during a retreat, during vacation bible classes or during Sunday morning church school with special emphasis (or a weekly theme) on getting connected through empowerment, encirclement, enrichment, self-help and interdependence methodologies. * Participates will receive a certificate of completion at the conclusion of the training session if 80 percent of the classes are attended, active participation is demonstrated, and lesson objectives are met. * Training sessions are lineal; therefore learners are encouraged to attend all sessions to maximize their learning effectiveness.	

Time	Teaching Activities	Resources
Discussion Questions	1. What are some roles/goals of the church, the Christian education ministry, leaders, and the laity? 2. In what ways are the aforementioned roles/goals functional and/or dysfunctional in this context? 3. What are ways of building a faith community that encourages and empowers leaders and the laity to grow spiritually and to work harmoniously utilizing Christian education approaches? 4. How can leaders and laity use each educational approach in ministry to empower and embrace others through Christian love?	

Where Do We Go From Here?

Social Consciousness for Leaders and the Laity in the 21st Century and Beyond

Main Idea

The main idea of this lesson is to teach leaders and the laity to recognize social changes that are reflected in their particular context. Learners will also recognize the value in Christian education that will assist leaders and the laity to face present and future social changes.

The Goal

The goal of this teaching session is to teach learners to utilize resources and qualified members, ministries, and local effective Christian referrals to embrace those who are seeking physical and spiritual guidance (wholeness). Learners will seek ways of compassionately embracing those who are wounded and lost in the congregation as well as in the local community.

Instructional Objectives

Upon completion of this lesson, the learners should be able to:

1. Discuss at least one social consciousness program in this context.

2. Name at least one effective transformative Christian educational methodology available to believers.

3. Name at least one way the learner will become personally invested in social consciousness during the next thirty days.

4. In a small group discussion, make a list of ways this church can address social consciousness/transformation.

Time	Teaching Activities	Resources
Opening **05 minutes**	The lesson opens with scripture and prayer; which will focus on effective social consciousness for this context. (The classroom(s) has been set up to facilitate class participation).	Podium, Tables, Chairs, and The Holy Bible Classroom(s)
Presenting the Subject 20 minutes	Opening remarks and an overview The facilitator will shows selected scenes from the DVD "Africans in America; America's Journey through Slavery," to facilitate discussion during the session.	Overview Television, DVD Player Cart Extension Cord
Exploring the Subject 45 minutes	Lecture and Discussions: • Define social consciousness/transformation and it's relevant to our context. • Learning to create an learning environment that promotes restoration amidst social hurts and pains where people are open to share their stories • Learner will be placed into small discussion groups and share positive ways this church can address social consciousness/transformation.	Tables, Chairs, a Podium, a Laptop Computer, a LCD Machine, and a Whiteboard. Notebook Papers and Pens
Conclud-ing the Session	Learners will present their discussion group list	

Time		Teaching Activities	Resources
Setting		The presenter with close will an overview (recap) of today's lesson; Christian education classroom(s) at	Tables, Chairs, a Podium, a Laptop Computer, a LCD Machine, and a Whiteboard Classroom(s)
Students		The students are members of YOUR CHURCH, and learners, preachers, teachers, and parishioners from local churches, and the community	
Notes		* This lesson is designed to be taught during; a mid-week bible study class, during a retreat, during vacation bible classes or during Sunday morning church school with special emphasis (or a weekly theme) on getting connected through empowerment, encirclement, enrichment, self-help and interdependence methodologies. * Participates will receive a certificate of completion at the conclusion of the training session if 80 percent of the classes are attended, active participation is demonstrated, and lesson objectives are met. * Training sessions are lineal; therefore learners are encouraged to attend all sessions to maximize their learning effectiveness.	

Pulling It Together

Discipleship and the Importance of Staying Connected
Utilizing Biblical Models: Establishing Spiritual Advisors

Main Idea

The main idea of this lesson is to introduce biblical models to learners who will demonstrate the importance of staying connected, and to empower leaders and laity to maintain continuity and to ensure open lines of communication.

The Goal

The goal of the teaching session is to understand the importance of staying connected as a body in Christ, to seek to establish a spiritual advisory group, and to make positive connections to tonight's and previous teaching sessions.

Instructional Objectives

Upon completion of this lesson, the learners should be able to:

1. Give a biblical scripture that reflects the importance of staying connected.

2. Name and give a brief explanation of a previous discussion topic.

3. Complete a post test

Time	Teaching Activities	Resources
Opening 05 minutes	The lesson opens with scripture and prayer; which will focus on staying connected to give God the glory as learners embrace spiritual empowerment, encirclement, and enrichment, amidst self-help and interdependence methodologies. The classroom(s) has been set up to facilitate class participation.	Podium, Tables, Chairs, and The Holy Bible
Presenting the Subject 10 minutes	Opening remarks and an overview of the lesson The facilitator will give a recap of previous lessons and their importance to learners. Lecture and Discussions: ✓ The relevance of pulling together and staying connected to leaders, laity and ministries through discipleship training.	Overview Laptop computer with a power point presentation, Tables, Chairs, a Podium, a Laptop Computer, and the LCD Machine

Time	Teaching Activities	Resources
Exploring the Subject 50 minutes	✓ Matthews 28: 18-20 (The Great Commission) ✓ 1 Corinthians 12:1 to 14:40 (A call to unity) ✓ Ephesians 4: 1-16 (Effectively building the body of Christ) ✓ Individualized and collected training sessions for further development ✓ The importance of establishing a spiritual advisors group. ✓ Unveiling and establishing YOUR CHURCH spiritual advisory group.	Notebook Papers and Pens Advisory Group Model
	An overview (recap) of the all lessons	
	Learners questions and answer session	Tables, Chairs, a Podium, a Laptop Computer, and the LCD Machine

Time	Teaching Activities	Resources
Concluding The session 10 minutes	Administer the post test	Post Test
The Post Test	Christian education classroom(s) at YOUR CHURCH The students are members of YOUR CHURCH, and learners, preachers, teachers, and parishioners from local churches and members of the community	
Students	* This lesson is designed to be taught during; a mid-week bible study class, during a re-treat, during vacation bible classes or during Sunday morning church school with special emphasis (or a weekly theme) on getting connected through empowerment, encircle-ment, enrichment, self-help and interdependence methodologies. * Participates will receive a certificate of completion at the completion of the training session if 80 percent of the classes are attended, active participation is demonstrated, and lessons objectives are met. * Training sessions are lineal; therefore learners are encouraged to attend all sessions to maximize their learning effectiveness.	

United We Stand and Divided We Shall Surely Fall

Guest Speaker and Presentation of Certificates

Main Idea

The main idea of this session is to give an overview of the teaching sessions. This session will also reemphasize the importance of staying connected in ministry and supporting the body of Christ in this context by committing to the spiritual advisory group. Lastly, Christian fellowship will be encouraged, and learners who completed and participated in at least 80 percent of the learning activities will receive their certificate of completion.

The Goal

The goal of this session is to encourage learners and participants (leaders, those in ministries, and the laity) to stay connected to the body of Christ and to one another.

Instructional Objectives

Upon completion of this lesson, the learners should be able to:

1. Verbally declare their commitment to:
   ✓ Christian education, and

   ✓ Encouraging effective biblical transformations
2. Verbally declare making positive relational connections to those in the church, the local community, and eventually those in all nations.

Time	Teaching Activities	Resources
Opening **05 minutes**	The session opens with scripture and prayer; which will give thanks to God for these learners and the positive impact they will make staying connected in a holistic environment that is conducive to biblical training and giving God the glory.	Podium, Tables, Chairs, and The Holy Bible
Presenting the Learners **15 minutes**	Opening Remarks	Tables, Chairs, a Podium, and Dinner
Guest Speaker **30 minutes**	The Facilitator will present the learners and discuss their relevance at Your Church and the importance of social consciousness for the 21st Century and Beyond. ((Dinner Served) Lessons overview and the concept of supporting the church's leadership	
Presentation **20 minutes**	**Topic** **United We Stand and Divided We Fall!** Presentation of certificates to learners	Podium, Tables, and Chairs
Closing Remarks **10 minutes**	Remarks	Certificates

Time	Teaching Activities	Resources
Setting	Prayer (commissioning leaders and laity)	Classroom
Students	Christian education classroom(s) at YOUR CHURCH	Classroom
	The students are members of YOUR CHURCH, and learners, preachers, teachers, and parishioners from local churches and members of the community	
	* Participates will receive a certificate of completion if 80 percent of the classes were attended, active participation demonstrated, and lessons objectives met.	
	Training sessions were lineal; therefore learners were encouraged to attend all sessions to maximize their learning effectiveness.	

APPENDIX E
MINISTRY MODEL A
AND
APPENDIX F
MINISTRY MODEL B

Who Is in Charge?

The preceding ministry models are presented as mere tools to assist the disconnected, engage conversation, and reconnect those who have been disconnected in ministry due to misunderstandings in ministry.

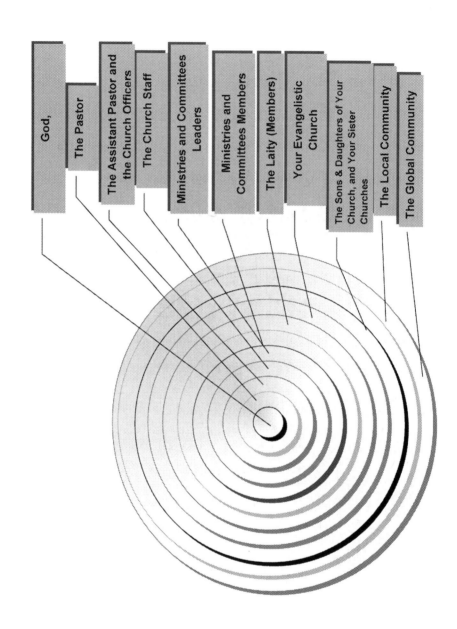

God,

The Pastor

The Assistant Pastor and the Church Officers

The Church Staff

Ministries and Committees Leaders

Ministries and Committees Members

The Laity (Members)

Your Evangelistic Church

The Sons & Daughters of Your Church, and Your Sister Churches

The Local Community

The Global Community

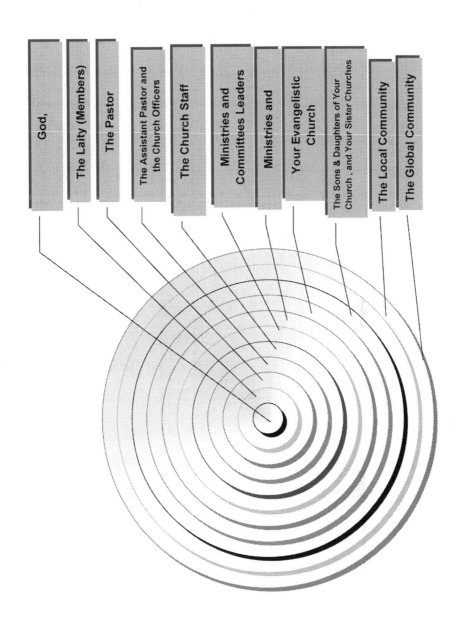

God,

The Laity (Members)

The Pastor

The Assistant Pastor and the Church Officers

The Church Staff

Ministries and Committees Leaders

Ministries and

Your Evangelistic Church

The Sons & Daughters of Your Church , and Your Sister Churches

The Local Community

The Global Community

Appendix G

Additional Questions to Evoke Awareness

The Pre-Test/The Post-Test

Additional Questions to Evoke Awareness

Pre-Test/Post-Test

Student's Identification Number: _____

Today's Date:_____

The questions in this section are confidential and may be used for gathering statistical data for the classes in this teaching session.

No student names or personal information will be given to any third parties without consent.

The questions in this section are questions to evoke conversations and help learners see negated situations they have caused another and/or have had perpetrated against them.

Please read the following questions/statements and select the answer that you believe most closely represents your belief and commitment to the body of Christ.

1. Select the best answer that describes your present church.

    a.(   ) Thriving toward restoration
    b.(   ) Thriving toward separation
    c.(   ) Thriving toward enriching, empowering, and embracing believers
    d.(   ) Thriving toward both A and C above

2. Do you believe the leadership and the congregation (laity) in the church you are attending is biblically connected or disconnected?

    a.(   ) Disconnected
    b.(   ) Connected
    c.(   ) Connected mentally but disconnected spiritually
    d.(   ) Disconnected mentally but connected spiritually

3. Do you believe that biblical transformation is relevant in addressing the needs of today's churches?

( ) Yes ( ) No ( ) Unsure

4. Do you believe leaders, those in ministries, and the laity should be connected to God and the body of Christ?

( ) Yes ( ) No ( ) Unsure

5. Do you believe negative attitudes and behavior traits are a problem in your church?

( ) Yes ( ) No ( ) Unsure

6. Is Christian education vital to your spiritual growth?

( ) Yes ( ) No ( ) Unsure

7. Is Christian education vital to leaders, those in ministry, and the church's growth?

( ) Yes ( ) No ( ) Unsure

8. Are positive attitudes and behaviors important to you in ministry?

( ) Yes ( ) No ( ) Sometimes

9. Is ethnicity and lineage in the body of Christ important to you?

( ) Yes ( ) No ( ) Sometimes

10. Do you believe open lines of effective communication is vital to the body of Christ being and staying connected in ministry?

( ) Yes ( ) No ( ) Unsure

11. In the Bible, Moses held group sessions when tensions were rising. Do you believe a spiritual advisory group of dedicated leaders and laity (ministry leaders and members) would assist in addressing and possibly resolving some problems before they escalate?

( ) Yes ( ) No ( ) Unsure

12. Do you believe biblical psychology is important in connecting (transforming) and reconnecting (revitalizing) leaders, those in ministry and the laity?

( ) Yes ( ) No ( ) Unsure

13. Do you believe biblical sociology is important in connecting (transforming) and reconnecting (revitalizing) leaders, those in ministry and the laity?

( ) Yes ( ) No ( ) Unsure

14. Do you believe social consciousness for the 21st century and beyond is important in connecting (transforming) and reconnecting (revitalizing) leaders, those in ministry and the laity?

( ) Yes ( ) No ( ) Unsure

15. Are you in a position to commit to effective and positive leadership?

( ) Yes ( ) No ( ) Unsure

16. Would you like to learn more about Christian education and staying connected to God and others in ministry after completing the "Getting Connected" training sessions?

( ) Yes ( ) No ( ) Unsure

17. Ongoing maintenance is vital in ministry and relationship. Do you believe quantifiable objectives and milestones that everyone

understands are important in staying connected and reconnecting leaders, those in ministry and the laity?

( ) Yes ( ) No ( ) Unsure

18. Do you know your role(s) and responsibility in the body of Christ?

( ) Yes ( ) No ( ) Unsure

19. Do you understand the role(s) and responsibilities of others in the body of Christ as a means of staying connected to God, to others in ministry, and to the laity?

( ) Yes ( ) No ( ) Unsure

20. Do you know the definition of a self-negated person?

( ) Yes ( ) No ( ) Unsure

21. Do you know the definition of cultural trauma?

( ) Yes ( ) No ( ) Unsure

22. Do you know the definition of liberation theology?

( ) Yes ( ) No ( ) Unsure

23. Do you know the definition of Black theology?

( ) Yes ( ) No ( ) Unsure

24. Do you know the definition of Christian education?

( ) Yes ( ) No ( ) Unsure

25. Do you know the definition of evangelism?

( ) Yes ( ) No ( ) Unsure

26. Do you know the definition of Diaspora?

( ) Yes ( ) No ( ) Unsure

27. Do you know the definition of self-help and Interdependence?

( ) Yes ( ) No ( ) Unsure

28. Do you know the definition of empowerment and encirclement?

( ) Yes ( ) No ( ) Unsure

29. Do you know the definition of spiritual care?

( ) Yes ( ) No ( ) Unsure

30. This Church is involved in the social well-being of its members.

( ) True ( ) False

31. You understand why it was important to strip Africans of their native languages, cultures, and other characteristics.

( ) True ( ) False

32. You are an African who lives in the Diaspora.

( ) True ( ) False

33. You know some steps that were employed to recreate an African into a Negro.

( ) True ( ) False

34. You know the impact of Willie Lynch's Speech on Americans.

( ) True ( ) False

35. You have read the Willie Lynch Speech.

    ( ) True ( ) False

36. Self-help and interdependence means receiving assistance from the church for my personal goals and gains.

    ( ) True ( ) False

37. You can trace your heritage back 150 years.

    ( ) True ( ) False

38. You can trace your heritage back 100 years.

    ( ) True ( ) False

39. You heritage (lineage) is important to you.

    ( ) True ( ) False

40. During Black History Month you celebrate African history.

    ( ) True ( ) False

41. During Black History Month you celebrate African American history.

    ( ) True ( ) False

42. Your spiritual heritage (lineage) is important to you.

    ( ) True ( ) False

43. Your heritage (lineage) is tied to your psychological well-being as a person.

(   ) True (   ) False

44. Do you understand assimilation and the melting pot theory?

(   ) Yes (   ) No (   ) Unsure

Bibliography

Akbar, Na'im, *Light from Ancient Africa* (Tallahassee, FL: Mind Production & Associates, 1994).

Broderick, Francis L., *W. E. B. Du Bois: Negro Leader in a Time of Crisis* (Palo Alto, CA: Stanford University Press, 1959).

Creswell, John W. *Research Design: Qualitative, Quantitative, and Mixed Methods Approaches* (Thousand Oaks, CA: Sage Publications, 2003).

Du Bois, W. E. B., *Du Bois on Sociology and the Black Community* (Palo Alto, CA: Stanford University Press, 2000).

Eyerman, Ron, *Cultural Trauma—Slavery and the Formation of African Americans Identity* (New York: Cambridge University Press, 2001).

Felder, Cain Hope, *Stony the Road We Trod: African American Biblical Interpretation* (Minneapolis: Fortress Press, 1991).

Griggs, Donald L., *Teaching Teachers to Teach—A Basis Manual for Church Teachers* (Nashville: Abingdon Press, 1980).

Harris, James H., *Pastoral Theology—A Black Church Perspective* (Minneapolis: Fortress Press, 1991).

———*Preaching Liberation* (Minneapolis: Fortress Press, 1995).
———*The Courage to Lead—Leadership in the African American Urban Church* (Lanham, MD: Rowman & Littlefield, 2002).

Hawkins, Thomas R. *The Learning Congregation—A New Vision of Leadership* (Louisville, KY: Westminster John Knox Press, 1997).

Hopkins, Dwight N. *Introducing Black Theology of Liberation* (Maryknoll, NY: Orbis Books, 1999).

Jacoby, Tamar, *Reinventing The Melting Pot: The New Immigrants and What It Means to Be American* (New York: Basic Books, 2004).

Johnson, Charles and Patricia Smith, *Africans in America—America's Journey Through Slavery* (New York: Harcourt Brace, 1998).

Kwame, Gyekye, *African Cultural Values—An Introduction* (Lansing, MI: Sankofa, 1996).

The Dalai Lama, *Toward a True Kinship of Faiths: How the World's Religions Can Come Together* (New York: Doubleday Religion, 2010).

Lebacoz, Karen and D. Driskill, *Ethics and Spiritual Care* (Nashville: Abingdon Press, 2000).

Manz, Charles. *The Leadership Wisdom of Jesus* (San Francisco: Berrett -Koehler, 1999).

Manz, Charles, Karen P. Manz, Robert D. Marx, and Christopher P. Neck, *The Wisdom of Solomon at Work* (San Francisco: Berrett -Koehler, 2001).

_____. *The New Super Leadership: Leading Others to Lead Themselves* (San Francisco: Berrett -Koehler, 2001).

Musser, Donald W. and Joseph L. Price, *A New Handbook of Christian Theology (Nashville: Abingdon Press)* 2002).

Perkins, James C., *Building Up Zion's Walls—Ministry for Empowering the African American Family* (Valley Forge, PA: Judson Press, 1999).

Reavis, Ralph, *Apostles of Self-Help and Independence: Chronicles of History* (African-Americans Publishers of Virginia, LLC. 1999).

Sanders, Boykin, *Blowing the Trumpet in Open Court—Prophetic Judgment and Liberation (Trenton: Africa World Press, Inc., 2002).*

Schaefer, Richard T. and Robert P. Lamm, *Sociology, Sixth Edition (New York: McGraw-Hill,1998).*

Seals, Eugene and Matthew Parker, *Called to Lead—Wisdom for the Next Generation of African American Leaders* (Chicago: Moody Press, 1995).

Seymour, Jack L., *Mapping Christian Education—Approaches to Congregational Learning* (Nashville: Abingdon Press, 1997).

Shawchuck, Norman and Roger Heuser, *Managing the Congregation* (Nashville: Abingdon Press, 1996).

Smiley, Tavis, *How to Make Black America Better: Leading African Americans Speak Out* (New York: Doubleday, 2001).

Thomas, Owen C. and Wondra, Ellen K., *Introduction to Theology* (Harrisburg: Morehouse Publishing, 2002).

Walinskas, Karl, *Getting Connected Through Exceptional Leadership* (Wilkes-Barre, PA: Kallisti Publishing, 2001).

Warren, Rick, *The Purpose Driven Life* (Grand Rapids, MI: Zondervan Press, 2002).

West, Cornel, *Race Matters* (New York: Vintage Books, 2001).

_____. *Keeping Faith: Philosophy and Race in America.* (New York: Routledge, 1993).

Wimberly, Anne Streaty, *Soul Stories—African American Christian Education* (Nashville: Abingdon Press, 1994).

Wright, H. Norman, *Making Peace with Your Past* (Ada, MI: Fleming H. Revell, 1985).

Wright, Walter C., *Relational Leadership—A Biblical Model for Leadership Service* (Carlisle, UK: Paternoster Press, 2000).

[1]   Seymour, Jack L. Mapping Christian Education, p. 93-128.